D1082073

THE PRESS
IN JAPAN TODAY...
A CASE STUDY

by edward p. whittemore

STUDIES IN INTERNATIONAL AFFAIRS NO. 1
Institute of International Studies, University of South Carolina

UNIVERSITY OF SOUTH CAROLINA PRESS—COLUMBIA—1961

FOREWORD

Demonstrations, disorder, and violence on the streets of Tokyo, and even in the Diet building itself, in May and June of 1960, evoked expressions of profound shock from the Western world, and particularly from the United States. Americans who watched their television sets or read press accounts of the mob actions were startled by the temporary collapse of what had seemed to be orderly democratic processes. There had been a general impression that affairs were proceeding smoothly in Japan, and in their preoccupation with the problems elsewhere in the Far East, Americans tended to take for granted or even forget about Japan.

Japan is far too important to be forgotten; developments there are likely, as they were twenty years ago, to be crucial in determining the course of international affairs. Preoccupation with the much-overplayed contest between Communist China and Democratic India has frequently resulted in too little attention to the achievements as well as the problems of post-World War II Japan. With remarkable energy and creativeness the Japanese have rebuilt their country and its economy into one of the wonders of the modern world. The island nation is now self-sufficient in foodstuffs for the first time in the twentieth century, her rate of industrial growth and its versatility are second to none, and despite a great poverty of natural resources, Japan has the highest standard of living in Asia. Japan has made the "great leap forward" in Asia and has provided the prime example of successful economic modernization, particularly in the field of agriculture.

[iii]

Yet with the rapid modernization and changes in the post-war period have come social and political tensions and the problems of handling a generation that has been set adrift by an abrupt disappearance of former principles and unifying themes. The events in the spring of 1960 highlighted these tensions and indicated that the foundations for responsible democracy are not as solid as many outsiders had been led to believe. A whole complex of historical, social, and political forces contributed to the tragic outburst. It would be a grave mistake to ignore these forces—which are still operative—and blame the events exclusively on Communist propaganda and mob manipulation, an explanation common in American press and television coverage, and one given by Prime Minister Kishi himself. On the other hand, there can be no question that the violence in Tokyo was in large part attributable to a long and concerted Communist psychological warfare campaign which took advantage of the complacency of the Liberal-Democratic Party and of the myopic naiveté of the Socialists.

In these terms the events in Tokyo take on a significance that extends beyond Japan. They constitute one of the most successful political warfare operations in recent times. Probably for the first time in history, the head of a major power was prevented from visiting in an allied country by organized and illegal mob action. The cancellation of President Eisenhower's visit to Japan brought discredit to the Japanese government, raised doubts about the future of Japanese democracy, set a precedent for future mob action, and demonstrated the ability of groups of professional agitators to interfere with normal processess of government at the behest of foreign powers. The events in the spring of 1960 also point up the crucial role of the capital city in Japan, just as later developments indicate the futility of attempting to judge the politics of the country as a whole on the basis of those of the capital.

There are other dimensions to the crisis in Japan which were inadequately covered in the United States. To comprehend the significance of the dispute over the ratification of the United States-Japanese security treaty, it is necessary to have a feeling for and understanding of Japanese youth and the role of the students and intellectuals in modern Japan. It is necessary to appreciate the role of compromise or "adjustment" and face saving in Japanese politics. And it would be the greatest of errors not to take into account the unique characteristics of the Japanese press and its power.

[iv]

It is from this last point of view that Edward P. Whittemore approaches the Treaty crisis and the events surrounding it. Mr. Whittemore brings to bear impressive qualifications for a case study of the Japanese press during the crisis. He was a copy editor for the *Japan Times,* the leading English-language newspaper in Japan. Personally present during the demonstrations, he mingled with the Japanese students and observed the various forces at work. A graduate of Yale University, Mr. Whittemore attended the Tokyo School of Japanese Language following service in Japan and Okinawa as an officer in the United States Marine Corps, and is fluent in Japanese. As his study indicates, he has a real feeling for the problems of modern Japan and depth in cultural understanding.

Mr. Whittemore's study is a significant contribution to scholarship on modern Japan and to an understanding of the events which took place in May and June 1960. His familiarity with Japanese journalism enables him to shed light on its current nature, its relation to the Treaty crisis, and the problem of responsibility of the press in one of the most literate societies in the world.

Mr. Whittemore visited the campus of the University of South Carolina at the start of the fall semester and met with student and faculty groups. All were impressed with his knowledge and insights on modern Japan. Members of the Department of International Studies, the Department of Political Science, and the School of Journalism met with him in a colloquium devoted to the present study, and there was agreement that this case study of the Japanese press constitutes a distinguished and ideal choice for the first of the Studies in International Affairs to be published by the Institute of International Studies of the University of South Carolina.

RICHARD L. WALKER,

James F. Byrnes Professor of International Relations.

Columbia, South Carolina,
November 28, 1961.

CONTENTS

I. INTRODUCTION

The Unique Position of Three Newspapers

In Japan 37 million newspapers are sold each day. This circulation is extraordinarily high and makes Japan one of the most newspaper-conscious countries in the world. Television has recently boomed—as an industry it ranks second only to that of the United States—but newspapers are still the primary media of news communication.

Because Japan is relatively small in land area, smaller than California, metropolitan newspapers are able to distribute nationally. Three dailies do—the *Asahi*, the *Mainichi*, and the *Yomiuri*. Together they account for 19 million newspapers each day, over half of all the newspapers published in the country. No other Japanese newspaper can approach these three in depth and breadth of reporting. In the resources they can bring to bear and in technical competence the three are in a class apart. In any section of the country there is the usual assortment of city and provincial papers, but none of them competes with the *Asahi, Mainichi,* and *Yomiuri* in the weight their coverage carries.

Further, the three papers also publish both morning and evening editions (that is, they publish editions continually from morning until night), so that a reader who subscribes to one is not apt to take an additional paper of equal or near-equal quality that would give him another slant on the news.

[1]

The result is that the three giant newspapers are something of an anomaly in international journalism. They are independent; they are mass papers of high quality; they operate without Government interference. Normally they report national and international news in a straightforward and perceptive manner; their front pages compare to those of the better newspapers of the world. In their features they tend to educate public taste rather than follow it. The profession of journalism is admired in Japan and the talent of its members is high. The public has great respect for the "big three" and they in turn profess to seek the highest ideals of libertarian journalism. What really sets them apart, however, is that in no other country with freedom of opinion is there such a concentration of influence in the public media.

An important question for Japan's new democracy is: how do the three national newspapers perform in their unique position of power?

In an attempt to answer the question, this study will examine the three papers in action during a crucial period, the spring of 1960 when the Revised Japan-United States Security Treaty was ratified. It is the best case for study in recent years, perhaps since the war, for several reasons: Japanese political institutions were under severe strain; passions were high and the Treaty "struggle," as the Japanese called it, had international as well as national significance. The "struggle" was a major test for the country's new, democratic press.

Background to the Treaty Revision

The original Japan-United States Security Treaty went into effect with the completion of ratification formalities of the peace treaty on April 28, 1952. Its primary purpose was to protect Japan against external aggression. Many Japanese felt Japan was not an equal party in the Treaty, however, and in 1958 negotiations opened to revise it.

In the revision the two nations agreed to cooperate in political and economic matters and the U.S. agreed to defend Japan militarily. One clause stated that there would be "prior consultation" with Japan before American forces stationed in Japan were deployed to other areas of the Far East, before American bases in Japan were used for purposes other than the defense of Japan proper, or before there were major equipment changes in U.S.

forces in Japan (such as the introduction of nuclear arms). Japan was not given veto power in these matters, but President Eisenhower assured Prime Minister Nobusuke Kishi that the U.S. would not act contrary to Japan's wishes. Kishi and Eisenhower publicized this fact by including it in a joint communique.

From the U.S. point of view the Revised Treaty recognized a new era of equal partnership and ended the last vestiges of the postwar relationship of conqueror and conquered. To the conservative Japanese Government and to much of the Japanese public it also meant that Japan was being treated with new respect in international councils. The Opposition in Japan, Socialists and Democratic-Socialists, had long opposed the original Treaty on the grounds that it gave Japan unequal status, but once a change for the better was in the offing they switched to opposing the revision also.

As for the Communist line, domestic and international, it had long been clear: the U.S. must have no commitment to defend Japan and no bases in Japan. Its real aim was to isolate Japan from the U.S. As the *Peking Review*, the official English-language weekly, put it in an editorial November 25, 1958: "Only an independent Japan can maintain democracy at home and follow a peaceful neutral policy in foreign affairs."

Communist China in particular waged a long propaganda battle against the Revised Treaty. Its main theme was that the people of Japan opposed the Treaty and that the Government, in defiance of the people, intended to use the Treaty to rebuild Japanese militarism. The Communist demand for a major internal Japanese crisis over the issue of the Treaty began early, a full two years before the new Treaty was signed and submitted to the Japanese Diet for consideration. The *Peking Review* of May 13, 1958 said that

> Japan, in short, is approaching the brink of an inevitable crisis . . . the Kishi Government has initiated a fascist policy of suppression and persecution.

Kishi personally was chosen by the Chinese Communists to be the symbol of the rebirth of evil in Japan, the evil that the Japanese "people" were opposing. On May 27, 1958, the *Peking Review* said that

> Kishi is not only suppressing the progressive forces and strangling democratic freedom in Japan, but also harbors imperialist designs against other countries.

The *People's Daily*, the *Pravda* of Communist China, added on November 1, 1958:

> Nobusuke Kishi has once again exposed his imperialist face. His is a grim imperialist visage which is no different from that of Hideki Tojo.

One way in which Mao Tse-tung's China made its line felt in Japan was to get Japanese visitors to sign "joint declarations." Thus a delegation from Sohyo, Japan's 3.5-million-member union federation, signed a joint statement on October 14, 1958, that would give

> expression to the common aspirations of the working class and the people of the two countries . . . the Japanese workers strongly protest against the aggressive military action of the U. S. war provocateurs.

The most effective declaration was gathered by the Chinese Communists in 1959 when delegations from both the Japanese Socialist and Communist Parties were visiting Peking. On March 7 of that year Inejiro Asanuma, the Secretary-General of the Socialist Party and the leading Opposition figure in Japan, put his signature to a statement that "U.S. imperialism is the common enemy of the Japanese and Chinese people." The statement had far-reaching effects.

For Asanuma, a popular and jovial non-theoretician from the right-wing of the Socialist Party, the statement was strangely out-of-cast. In Japan only the doctrinaires of the Left appreciated it; for the most part it was received harshly and proved detrimental both to Asanuma's political prestige and to the Socialist claim to neutrality in the cold war. It plainly did not help the Socialists' or Asanuma's cause, but whether or not Asanuma would have liked to repudiate it later, he never did. The "common enemy" statement remained a clever achievement and weapon for the Communists.[1]

Despite the demands by the Japanese far Left and by Communist propaganda abroad that a political crisis be precipitated over the Treaty, such a crisis failed to materialize during the negotiating phase. In the course of two years Ambassador Douglas

---

[1] As for Asanuma, his unfortunate career ended a year and half later: while speaking on television to millions of viewers he was stabbed to death by an 18-year-old fanatic, who said he acted because he believed "irresponsible Leftism" was bringing the country to ruin.

MacArthur II and Foreign Minister Aiichiro Fujiyama met 22 times, and in January 1960, Prime Minister Kishi went to Washington to sign the Treaty. 1960 was also the year of the centennial anniversary of Japan-United States relations and many ceremonies had been planned. President Eisenhower's visit to Japan in June, the first by an American President in office, would climax the celebration along with the new Treaty of accord. Kishi flew back to Japan and in February presented the Treaty to the Lower House of the Diet for ratification.

At the time Kishi's conservative party, the Liberal-Democrats, held 283 seats in the Lower House as opposed to the 162 seats held by the Socialists and the Democratic-Socialists. The Opposition had mounted a demonstration in November 1959 and followed with several others in the winter and early spring of 1960. But support for the demonstrations was restricted mainly to the organized Left—the militant wings of some unions and a minority of activist students—and did not arouse any general enthusiasm against the Treaty. It appeared that after several months of routine debate and bickering the Lower House would ratify the Treaty without incident.

But an unforeseen turning point came in May when the U-2 was downed in the USSR and the summit conference in Paris failed to bring the "relaxation of tension" for which so many had hoped. Particularly in Japan the two events greatly influenced national affairs.

U-2s had been based in Japan for some time. Once one had crash-landed near an airfield and the peculiar design and markings had aroused much curiosity in the press, which referred to the planes mysteriously as the "black jets." [2] The Socialists had from time to time brought up the issue of the "black jets" and queried the Government on them, but the Government and the U.S. Embassy had answered that they were weather-reconnaissance planes and the matter had not been pressed. In May, when the country discovered the real purpose of the U-2's, Japanese-United States relations suffered an important setback. And when the failure of the summit followed immediately thereafter, general apprehension over U.S. bases in Japan increased.

Because of these two events and the resulting uncertainty over what the next months would bring, doubts over a ten-year military pact with the U.S. soared.

---

[2] The first description of a U-2 to appear in the U. S. was copied from a year-old Japanese magazine.

In this setting the Prime Minister took the country by surprise by dramatically using his party's majority to force a vote in the Diet on May 19. The Treaty was voted through the Lower House, but demonstrations, riots, and the cancellation of Eisenhower's trip followed.

II. THE NATURE OF
THE JAPANESE PRESS

Influence on Public Opinion

The press was not a bystander to this turbulence. As would be expected of the press in a free country, it took a vigorous part. It opposed the Government but without supporting the Opposition outright. Instead it found fault with both and in varying degrees criticized both. It claimed throughout the Treaty struggle that it was representing public opinion, which appeared to be dissatisfied with both political protagonists—the Government and the Socialists.

"Public opinion" can be nebulous, however, and in a country where independent thought is still pubescent it becomes even more obscure. Japanese editors and journalists are among the more politically articulate in their country. One would expect them not only to reflect public opinion but to take part in forming and leading it, which of course they do.

The exact role of the newspapers in forming public opinion is probably impossible to appraise. The effect the press has in any country is indistinct and a definitive assessment of its weight cannot be given. We know that the 19 million newspapers of the big three national papers must have an important relation to public opinion; and because the Japanese are avid readers, have a near-perfect literacy rate, and tend to revere the printed word, the influence is considerable. On the other hand, there is no way to guage whether the press descriptions of what is happening are any more important, ultimately, than the word-of-mouth accounts of the marketplace. Furthermore in the case of Japan, where the tradition of listening to one's elders still lives, the opinions of a superior—an office executive, a shop foreman, a village rice dealer— may be more significant in forming opinions in the end than either what is heard in the marketplace or read in the newspaper.

One aspect of the relationship of press and public is not obscure, however, and that is that Tokyo is so much the political, social, and cultural center of Japan that its mood tends to predominate in the national papers. Although the "big three" publish simultaneously in various parts of the country, their main offices are in Tokyo and their direction and stimuli come from there.

This is not unusual; it might happen in any country where the capital far excels its other cities. But in a country such as Japan where there is a wide divergency between urban and rural ways— in concepts they are often more than a generation apart—it is unusually significant. It means that the editors of the national papers, in interpreting "public opinion," have the tendency to judge the national mood by what they see around them in the streets of Tokyo. This can, of course, be extremely misleading. Tokyo has over one-tenth of the nation's population and is the largest city in the world; it is an important part of the national electorate and in most ways its leader. But it is still only one part of the national electorate and it represents specifically the sentiments of *urban* Japan. At least now and in the near future, the national mood, especially in politics, is something else again.

This is made perfectly clear by the historical record: five months after Tokyo had been shaken by huge demonstrations and violent riots against the Government, the Government Party was returned to power in a general election with 57.6 per cent of the popular vote and a postwar record majority in the Lower House (296 out of 467 seats). Obviously nation-wide "public opinion" had not been well-represented by the spring events in Tokyo.[1]

This study, however, does not attempt to assess the exact influence of the Japanese press on public opinion. It is a study of the *responsibility* of the press in both its "objective" news columns

---

[1] Because of widespread revulsion to the violence fostered by the Opposition during the Treaty struggle, it can be assumed that the disorders in May and June to some extent worked to the advantage of the Government in the November election. But the main difference between the anti-Government action in Tokyo in the spring—the sentiment the press had pictured as national— and the strong vote *for* the Government in the fall, was the will of the rural populace. This the press had largely ignored.

and its editorial commentary. It will be assumed that the press is substantially influential both in what the public accepts as facts and in the way the public interprets these facts. Admittedly these assumptions are unprovable, but significant factors support each one.

First, two aspects of the national papers cited before—their combination of excellence with a mass audience and of morning with evening editions—mean these papers are for many people the only authoritative source of news. Second, many Japanese are unused to arriving at opinions independently and rely heavily on others to make interpretations for them. The national papers are known to be powerful enough in their own right not to be bought on an issue by political parties or vested interest groups. In the public's view, therefore, the papers are considered objective and unbiased. Thus the facts reported in the big three national papers often become the facts accepted, and their interpretation of the facts is likly to become the general interpretation.

The Criteria of Responsibility

To assess the degree of responsibility of the national papers in Japan some discussion of the function of a free press is necessary.

Japan's press, like that of the U.S. and most democracies, operates under a libertarian theory that is largely undefined. In some areas of the theory there is consensus: for example, it is almost always assumed that the state and its legal apparatus must protect the reputations of individuals. But it is generally not assumed that the state can protect its own reputation (an important departure between the libertarian and authoritarian theories of the press).

Most advocates of the libertarian concept would further agree that it is the "right and duty of the press to serve as an extralegal check on government." In fact there is a strong tradition for the press in a democracy to be especially on guard against the government: "Because liberalism was forced to struggle for several centuries against authoritarianism, it [the press] considered the established government the greatest enemy." [2]

This is less true today in the older democratic societies, where liberals (20th century ones) now consider the established govern-

---

[2] Cf. *Four Theories of the Press*, by Fred Siebert *et al.*, University of Illinois Press, Urbana, 1956.

ment their strongest ally, but it was true before and is true in a still young democracy, such as Japan.

The disagreements in the libertarian concept arise when restrictions on the freedom of the press are considered. On this issue there is little consensus except on such specific points as individual libel and obscene materials. It is difficult to determine, for example, where the state is illegitimately protecting its own reputation through sedition and libel laws and where it is legitimately safeguarding public order by suppressing incitations to riot. Under the libertarian concept the former is a restriction on the freedom of the press and the latter is not. This is true in Japan as it is in the U.S. But in reaction to the very recent history of government interference and authoritarianism in Japan, the legal interpretations on freedom of the press are likely to be more liberal there than they are in the U.S.

The Japanese press has itself defined a code to serve as its standard. It is known as "The Canons of Journalism" and has been adopted by the Japan Newspaper Publishers and Editors Association. Section II, on news reporting and editorial writing, reads:

> The freedom of news reporting and editorial writing should be bound by the following voluntary restraints:
> 1) The fundamental rule for news reporting is to convey facts accurately and faithfully.
> 2) In reporting news, the personal opinion of the reporter should never be inserted.
> 3) In treating news, one should always remember and be strictly on guard against the possibility of such news being used for propaganda purposes.

Section V of the code is entitled "Tolerance." It reads:

> A fundamental principle of democracy recognizes the freedom of individual assertions and counter-assertions, and should be reflected clearly in the editing of newspapers. The tolerance such as to allot just as much news in introducing and reporting the policies which a newspaper opposes as it would give to others which it supports is the fundamental character of democratic newspapers.

These are admirable standards and good criteria for viewing the performance of the press. Since they are professed by Japanese journalism, the performance of the national papers and the degree of their responsibility during the Treaty struggle can be measured against them.

In the case of Japan, a young democracy, the "extralegal check" that the press provides has to be further examined. For although it is not curious that the press in a country only recently emerged from authoritarianism should in general be highly suspicious of the Government, a situation where *all* the major newspapers are hostile to the Government is unusual.

This would be unlikely to happen in the West, where except on the most extreme issues at least one leading newspaper can be expected to favor what two or three others oppose. There is therefore a degree of balance and the public is usually presented both sides of any debate. In Japan, however, this is not the case. The "big three" in concert regularly oppose the Government. During the Treaty struggle, in fact, their opposition went beyond suspicion of the Government and amounted to an adamant campaign against it.

Thus in a crucial debate over whether the Government would stand or fall and whether Japan would be aligned with the West or move towards neutralism, the Government had not one major defender, or even spokesman, in the national press. To understand this the Japanese concept of political leadership and the history of Japanese newspapers during the Occupation have to be taken into account.

The Anti-Government Bias

The first important newspapers in Japan were Government-subsidized journals which began in the 19th century when Japan ended its feudal era. Soon individuals and groups founded other papers, but because authority at that time was monolithic, the non-Government papers were almost by definition anti-Government in their views. Throughout the early 20th century this tradition continued and became a habit. An attack on the ruling forces and a strong anti-Government position were the signs of an independent newspaper; an "impartial" newspaper was a newspaper that opposed the Government.

During the 1920s there was a brief, relatively liberal period in Japanese society, and the press was able to develop an even greater freedom of comment. But soon the racist and ultra-nationalist reaction followed and the press became subservient to the militarists. In the 1930s, sometimes through coercion and sometimes through sympathy, it gave up its independence to serve the national cult. Outright criticism of the Government ended, and eventually there came censorship and complete Government control.

In 1945 the press reestablished itself as an "unbiased" critic independent of particular political party programs. In other words the press intended to speak out against the ruling forces "in the name of the people." Until 1952 there had been ruling forces above the people: first an oligarchic group, then a military one, and finally a foreign occupation. But in 1952 the "ruling forces," legally for the first time, became the people as a whole.

To decree democracy and practice it are two different affairs, of course, and the theory and the fact are still separate in Japan. The press, like other sections of Japanese society, has had difficulty accommodating itself to the new principles. It suffers from not having built its new freedom itself, from having received it during the Occupation. Since the years of experience are few there are inevitable gaps in the democratic tradition. Where the gaps appear the press falls back on what it knows—its own history. The history was a peculiar one and has proved to be influential. Today it helps explain why the Japanese press unconsciously believes a bias against the Government is "unbiased" journalism. The unspoken creed is: all political parties should be equally criticized, but the Government Party more equally than others.

Concomitant with this is what a logician might call the fallacy of misplaced concreteness. It becomes apparent not in what the press criticizes, but in how it criticizes. For example, since the Japanese press is "unbiased," it will not support a political party at election time or a partisan (that is, party) position any time except on a monetary, *ad hoc* basis (party organs excepted). Instead, all politicians and parties are measured against an ideal norm, and any political figure who deviates from the ideal norm is criticized.

In theory this may sound something like the universal aim of independent journalism. In fact, however, it is not; rather it is a manifestation of a Japanese characteristic—an identification of relative values with absolute ones. What actually happens is that since no politician or party can equal the ideal, all politicians and parties are criticized in proportion to their prominence. The prime minister, as the most prominent politician of all, is criticized more than anyone else regardless of who he is. He is responsible for the whole nation and, therefore, for the always-existing divergency between the actual and ideal state of affairs.

In political life today the transmutation of relative into absolute values may be the result of the peculiar evaluation of the emperor from obscurity to omnipotence at the time of the Meiji Restoration in the 19th century. At that time, as a convenience for uniting the country and bringing it out of feudalism, the emperor was transformed into a divinity embodying the state and the race. Subsequently everything was accomplished in his name, in theory, by him personally. However, there was no tradition for this: for a thousand years the emperor had been of no consequence; since the 9th century the country had been run first by powerful court families and later by military dynasties. Politically, as in other ways, expediency had ruled and there had been no absolutes, least of all in theory.

In the 19th century the emperor was apotheosized—for expedient reasons—but at the same time he was conceptualized as an absolute. In practice he was not anything of the sort; real power belonged not to the emperor but to his "advisors"—elder statesmen, generals, financial magnates—who made up the oligarchy and ran the nation in a very pragmatic way. When affairs of state went badly it had nothing to do with the emperor; the "advisors" were criticized and held responsible because of the bad "advice" they had given to the diety. Historically an absolute is out-of-place in Japanese thinking. A political absolute (the restored emperor) was a makeshift in Japanese history that could only be accepted by the Japanese if it was not held responsible for anything that actually determined history. Furthermore, because the Japanese find little sustenance in abstractions, the emperor-absolute eventually created as many problems as it initially solved.[3]

Since the war the "people" have replaced the emperor, and all political action is now theoretically carried out in the name of the people. But the old thought pattern lingers—responsibility and the pretense of power are never found in the same place. Thus

---

[3] The young patriots and militarists who assassinated cabinet members and prime ministers in the 1930s always moved under the convenient excuse of "serving the emperor's true will." Since the will did not really exist, anyone could say he was acting in its name. And because their motives were "pure," that is, to serve the emperor, they could flagrantly disregard the law of the land, even commit murder, and still expect and receive much sympathy from the general public.

The best example of the unconscious unacceptance of the emperor-absolute, however, was the extraordinary inability of the Japanese to define or identify the emperor. Even at the height of the prewar racist cult the nationalist philosophers were never able to be more definite than describing the emperor as "everything." Explanations would soon lapse into more tangible metaphors which had some meaning, such as the father-son relationship, and which were in no way connected with absolutes.

just as the "advisors," and not the emperor, were held absolutely responsible for the state of the nation before the war, so today the Prime Minister, and not the people, is often held absolutely responsible. Even when the situation is not this extreme, the press, in any case, would obviously be accused of abandoning its ideals if it ever supported a Prime Minister.

The extreme concern for "responsibility" is itself indicative of the confusion of relative and absolute values. One notices throughout the editorials of May and June 1960 a continual, almost daily, plea for someone to take responsibility for what is happening. The national papers found that both the minority party, with its obstructionist tactics, and the majority party, with its overbearing methods, were in varying degrees responsible for the growing conflict and disorder. Despite their anti-Government predilections, the "big three" occasionally accused the minority party of being as guilty as the majority party in trespassing against parliamentary democracy. Yet although the minority party was a "problem," ultimate responsibility always belonged to the majority party. Even if both sides committed the same act and diverged from the ideal in the same way, their responsibility was not considered equal. The majority party held two-thirds of the seats in the Diet; at least two-thirds of the responsibility was therefore theirs.

As the *Mainichi* said in an editorial June 5:

> A unilateral Diet leads to a rejection of parliamentary policies. Of course the Socialist Party's refusal to deliberate is also responsible for the present situation, but . . . the main responsibility belongs to the party with the absolute majority.

In the same way the *Asahi*, in an editorial May 24, said the Socialists were "not correct" for refusing to take part in the Upper House plenary session then being held, but it did not criticize them because, it asserted, the "reckless action" of the Government had created the problem.

Unions and the Occupation

When the war ended in 1945, the press was nothing more than an organ of the militarist government. It had grown unused to printing the truth or seeking facts. The American effort to democratize the newspapers began at once and went through several stages.

Immediately after the war many of the leading editors were purged as reactionaries. Some were tried as war criminals and others were merely forced to retire from an active role. All of them had to sell their controlling interests, generally to the employees of their newspapers. In addition the Occupation encouraged the growth of newspaper unions as a liberal force, so that where former ownership remained it still would not be able to act autocratically. The new unions were organized on the enterprise basis: all employees of a newspaper joined one union—editorial workers, pressmen, and cafeteria help alike.

The Communists enjoyed a favored position in the first days of the Occupation. General Douglas MacArthur's headquarters allowed them to function freely, and because they had the reputation of having actively opposed the militarists in the 1930s and of having gone to jail for it, the public viewed them as popular figures. The Communists were quick to take advantage of the friendly atmosphere, especially in the rapidly expanding union field where often they were the only group able to provide experienced leadership. The enterprise unions springing up in the newspapers were ideal targets for penetration, for with only a majority of the manual workers behind them, Leftists could dictate to the union and through the union control the editorial content of the paper. Leftist influence was soon felt in all the papers, and at least in one union, that of the *Yomiuri*, Leftists won control.

The *Yomiuri's* owner at the end of the war had been one of those forced to sell his controlling shares. He had appointed a moderate liberal as his successor, but when the newspaper's union came under Leftist control, the union elected one of its own representatives to serve as the paper's managing editor. The managing editor subsequently began to run the paper, disregarding the real editor, and a battle developed between the Leftist union on the one hand and the publisher and his editor on the other. The contest for editorial control of the *Yomiuri*—by union or by publisher —became a test case for postwar Japanese journalism.

For weeks there were strikes by the union and lockouts by the publisher. Finally after several days of violence the publisher triumphed in June 1946. A number of extreme Leftists were fired, including the managing editor appointed by the union. The incident marked a shift away from employee control as the Occupation tried to bring the newspapers back from the far Left position of the early postwar months.[4]

In May 1948 the newspaper unions withdrew from the Leftist-controlled National Congress of Industrial Unions, but in June 1949 the Occupation authorities found it necessary to block an attempted Communist takeover of Kyodo, Japan's leading wire service, by ordering the company's directors to fire a number of Communists. The Communist effort to influence the press, in other words, did not end simply because of serious setbacks during the Occupation.

The Government also tried its hand at limiting the freedom of the press. In January 1949, incumbent Diet members, hoping to benefit from a ban on campaigning by their lesser known opponents, passed a law eliminating many forms of electioneering. The law was not aimed primarily at the press, but the Government interpreted it as meaning that newspapers could not support any particular party or candidate. Two newspapers brought to account by the Government were the *Yomiuri*, by then moderate in outlook, and *Akahata*, the organ of the Japanese Communist Party. But Occupation headquarters said the Government's interpretation of the law was unconstitutional and support of candidates became legal again.

Democratization of the press during the Occupation was largely successful. The war-time ownership was broken, as was the subsequent control by Leftists. The Government was kept out until the press had developed enough to protect its own interests. Enterprise newspaper unions and their influence, however, have continued.

Today each newspaper's union is made up of almost all employees, section heads excepted. The three national newspapers are owned entirely by their employees, and although not all employees own stock, they are all eligible to apply for it as it becomes available. In the *Mainichi* there are no substantial shareholders; in the *Yomiuri* only the publisher holds a substantial amount—about 20 per cent. In the *Asahi* two families own about 60 per cent of the stock, but there too the employees in their other role as shareholders play an important part.

Elections to the leading positions on the papers are held every two years, and votes can be cast by proxy. As would be expected in Japan, seniority is significant, but popularity with fel-

---

[4] Cf. Wm. J. Coughlin, *The Conquered Press*, Pacific Books, Palo Alto, California, 1952.

low employees is also important because of the ownership structure. The potential influence of the union in determining editorial lines is apparent, as is the potential of a well-organized bloc among the employees.

The unions of the national papers are all members of *Shimbun Roren* (The Japan Federation of Newspapers Workers' Unions), which in turn is a member of Sohyo, the national, Left-leaning federation of unions that along with the Socialists led the campaign against the Treaty. Of course the loyalty the average reporter feels toward *Shimbun Roren* (and Sohyo) does not come close to approaching the loyalty he feels for his newspaper. But the very fact that he is a member of a union, and that the union is an active affiliate of one of the two leading forces of the political Opposition, is noteworthy.

Of more significance than the unions in influencing news coverage is the Japan Congress of Journalists (JCJ), a member of the International Organization of Journalists, which has its headquarters in Prague and most of its members from the Communist bloc. In the past the JCJ has led in such efforts as urging the press, unsuccessfully, to call Communist China *chukoku* (the historical name for China), rather than *chukyo* (which means Communist China). In May 1959, the JCJ issued a statement saying that a "revision of the Security Treaty which will menace peace and independence should not be permitted," and in July, it co-sponsored with *Shimbun Roren* a rally of journalists against the Treaty. In the same year it also published a pamphlet against the Treaty.

Its clearest statement on the role of its members, however, came just prior to a major strike and demonstration against the Government on June 4, 1960. The JCJ issued an appeal to its members that ended:

> Let us answer the expectations of the masses on June 4 with our news stories! Let newspapers carry the voice of the people who are giving support to the strike!

At the time of the Treaty struggle the JCJ had about 1,600 members, of whom over 1,200 were employed in the Tokyo metropolitan area. Among the three national papers the *Asahi* had by far the most with 242 members. The *Mainichi* had 73 members and the *Yomiuri* had 49. The *Asahi*, in fact, had the highest number of any of the news media in the country. Kyodo, the wire service, was second in the country with 187 members.

Although the three national papers all opposed the Government with equal vigor, the record of the news reporting during the Treaty crisis shows that the *Asahi* often omitted an event, or slanted an event, that the *Mainichi* and *Yomiuri* reported more factually. Except in one or two cases where articles were intentionally slanted in the *Asahi,* the differences between the *Asahi* and the other two papers were a matter of degree. But the slight variation is so often apparent that a regular pattern is discernible. After all, the purpose of the JCJ members, rather than factual reporting, was to "answer the expectations of the masses . . . with our news stories." The *Asahi* has twice the number of JCJ members as the other two papers combined. It is understandable that on the *Asahi* a number of editors and reporters often found factual coverage inadequate.

III. THE PRESS
AND "ADJUSTMENT"

The Case Made for Extra-Parliamentary Action

The national newspapers were sympathetic with the Socialist claim that the forced Diet vote on the Treaty was a "tyranny of the majority," a phrase once used in the United States by John C. Calhoun. Such a tyranny is a possibility in a democracy, especially in an inexperienced democracy where the Opposition is perennially out of power and there is a history of Government authoritarianism. A case for it might be built around Kishi's handling of the Treaty. The issue is complicated, however, by the peculiar Japanese concept of decision-making.

Traditionally in Japan, views are not allowed to clash; instead they are "adjusted" with as deep a façade of harmony as possible. Geography, the Confucian ethic, and an ingrained sense that power is deceptive and hidden may be involved; in any case, the term is used so often in Japanese political arguments it must be reckoned with. During May and June of 1960, it appeared again and again in the press: the Government Party had to "adjust" its arrogant stance; the Opposition Party had to "adjust" its extreme antagonism; the Treaty had to be "adjusted" to reflect public opinion. At first these suggestions might seem so vague as to be meaningless, but to the Japanese editorial writers doggedly churning them out they were sound proposals. To them an "adjustment" of opposing views is the pragmatic solution for political crises.

The reasoning is autochthonous. For a Japanese it is impossible to stand up, be tested, and be utterly rejected without at the same time being disgraced. Yet this is what happens to minority party parliamentarians if a bill before the Diet has not first been "adjusted" to include at least some of their opinions. The changes may be largely inconsequential, but if there are none whatsoever the situation is unbearable. When there has not been even token "adjustment," the minority party in the eyes of the nation is proved completely ineffectual. In other words, they have not only been defeated but shamefully defeated, and the average Japanese would probably agree this sort of disgrace is severe and should be avoided. On the other hand, if there has been "adjustment" of some kind, one-third of the Diet members and the electorate they represent need not feel embittered and forced to recoup their losses in some dramatic gesture (such as massive demonstrations). If a few of their opinions have been incorporated, their inadequacy is less than final, and it then becomes possible for them to rationalize, a standard and acceptable response.

Kishi, whose actions during the spring of 1960 had become remarkably like those of a Western leader elected by an overwhelming popular mandate, was uncompromising with the parliamentary minority opposing the Treaty—the Socialists, the Democratic Socialists, and the dissident factions within his own party.[5] There

---

[5] Japanese political party life centers around "factions," each with a strong leader. Sometimes the factions are vaguely ideological, but their basic causes are the Japanese tradition of belonging to a group, and more particularly, the tradition of attaching oneself to a person more advanced in power or ability. A Diet member gives his loyalty to his faction leader, voting as his leader says, and in turn the leader helps the protégé on to success. The custom is an old one and operates in business and education as well. It is rather like the master-apprentice relationship practiced by artisans in medieval Europe. In the conservative (Liberal-Democratic) party it works as follows: when a new cabinet is in the making the potential Prime Minister (the strongest of the present group of faction leaders) negotiates with the other faction leaders to see what he must give them for their support. The Foreign Minister has recently not been a faction leader (perhaps because that post is not independent enough), but the other leading cabinet positions are distributed to leaders according to the strength of their factions. Recognizing that the business community is the party's financial support, the party generally allows the second strongest faction leader to be Minister of International Trade and Industry. When Kishi was Prime Miinster, Hayato Ikeda had the second biggest faction and was Minister of International Trade and Industry; when Kishi resigned, Ikeda became Prime Minister and Eisaku Sato, Kishi's half-brother, took Ikeda's old job. If a faction leader dies or retires, there is chance for realignments and for the more capable to set up their own factions. The Socialist Party has not been in power except for a few months in 1947 as part of a coalition government, but it too is made up of factions. However, in the Socialist Party there tend to be more ideological differences among factions than in the conservative party.

was no "adjustment" of the Treaty he had negotiated; instead the police were used to allow the undissenting factions of his party to pass the Treaty exactly as he had negotiated it and exactly as he had first presented it to the Diet for consideration. If his mandate had been as outstanding as Franklin Roosevelt's in 1932 or Charles De Gaulle's in 1958, it is conceivable this might not have brought the reaction it did, even though there is the Japanese habit of "adjustment." A substantial segment of his party's support, however, comes from rural areas that are politically unconscious and vote on traditionalist lines. Further, there was disagreement, reluctance, and open hostility among the centrist elements of his own party. Some of this, as in Ichiro Kono's case, was obviously nothing more than part of the struggle for power within the party. But in the case of the Miki-Matsumura faction the disagreement was based on real issues.[6] To many in his own party the ten-year term of the Treaty seemed an over-long commitment for a country just beginning to formulate an independent foreign policy. In short, despite the vast numerical superiority of the Government Party in the Diet, Kishi's mandate to commit the nation to his policy was far from overwhelming among those politically literate. As it happened, his Western-style use of the Government Party's majority was unable to overcome the native need for "adjustment."

The press laid great emphasis on the fact that the vote on the Treaty was "unilateral." To them it was unilateral for two reasons: first, because only the majority party participated in it, and second, because the majority prior to the vote had refused consultation and compromise with the minority. The press considered the first action "unfortunate," but it was apparent that the Socialists, by being obstructionist and holding a sit-down in the Diet, were as much to blame as anyone else for letting that happen. The reaction in the press to this was rational and one of dismay.

The second action incensed the press because it disregarded the Japanese principle that lies behind "adjustment"—the need for total participation in decisions, that is, conformity. Their reaction to this "unethical," un-Japanese act of Kishi was emotional. It was the real cause of their charge of "tyranny of the majority."

---

[6] Two factions of Kishi's party, those of Tanzan Ishibashi and of Takeo Miki and Kenzo Matsumura, opposed the Treaty in the form in which Kishi presented it and in the way he forced it through the Diet. They absented themselves from the Diet during the vote. Both were small groups. The Kono faction attacked Kishi on various matters but voted for the Treaty; it was a much larger group than either that of Ishibashi or of Miki and Matsumura.

In Japanese terms, although probably not in Western ones, there had been such a tyranny.

In other words, it is inherent in Japanese thinking that social contracts are multilateral or non-existent. When social contracts exist they are immediate, concrete, and binding, but they cannot be generalized or abstracted. By extension this applies also to political contracts such as the Diet, where a majority and minority must work with one another. Together they form the Diet, the national will; separately they represent only partial, incomplete opinions, for the will of the people, by nature of the Japanese stress on totality, is complete, "adjusted," and conforming. Each of the two elements that make up the Diet, the stronger and the weaker, are under obligation not only to those who elect them but to each other, as if the arrangement were a covenant. If one party breaks the covenant—the Socialist Party by refusing to compromise and vote, or the Government Party by refusing to compromise and forcing a vote—the size of the Government Party's majority is not the significant factor. The essential point is that the Diet has not represented the will of the people because it has ceased to represent totality.

Within this view, since the multilateral contract has been broken by one of the parties (the press believed the Government, and especially Kishi, were responsible for the break), the other party is more or less free to act as it can, using whatever tools are at hand. At this point a demonstration against the Diet is not an attack on the national parliament, because the Diet ceased to be national when its covenant of totality was broken. A new "adjustment" to reestablish totality is necessary, but until that happens the national will of the people is fragmented and found in many places—among Socialist leaders demonstrating in the streets as well as among Government leaders sitting in the Diet building. In short, the Diet, in Japan today, as a national parliament, is not yet an institution able to transcend its elements or its traditional view of their function. A *modus operandi,* Japanese fashion, attempts to achieve totality through a multilateral contract. From the standpoint of autochthonous political views, therefore, the early Socialist demonstrations were as reasonable to the press as Kishi's Western-style posturing was unreasonable.

War Fear

The dismay caused in Japan by the U-2 incident and the failure of the Paris summit meeting, mentioned before, should be re-emphasized, for the fact is that the Treaty could not have caused such unrest in Japan, had it not been for those two events.

Both were manifestations of the cold war. Relevant to this is the fact that as a result of their tragedies in World War II the Japanese, as individuals and as a nation, are probably as pacifistic as any people in the world. Their aversion to war is so strong that it makes little difference to many Japanese whether war is a means or an end. It may be, as is sometimes said, that in the end the Japanese suffered more from World War II than the people of any other nation. But even that cannot explain their reasoning on war. On the other hand, the Japanese are an unusually pragmatic people; they are also a second-rate power, aware of it, and willing to be one. Without delusions of international grandeur, and without having a bent for living by ideologies, their pragmatism holds sway.

We should add that they are, as a nation, unaware of the scope and intensity of the struggle between international Communism and the United States and its allies. Japan's international experience is recent, after all, and shows a painful naïveté—imitation rather than understanding during the 19th century, arrogance that ignored understanding during the prewar era, acquiescence without understanding during the Occupational era. Today, because many Japanese do not fully understand their own freedoms, there is insufficient understanding of why there is a cold war between the free countries and Communism. Their pacifism, in short, is the result of both experience and a lack of experience; it is pragmatic yet unrealistic. Consequently there was great optimism over the Paris summit conference. The "spirit of Camp David" for many months had had a mythopoeic effect on the Japanese. Intellectuals especially expected a sudden and dramatic détente to come out of Paris, and when the U-2 crashed and the summit meeting collapsed their disillusionment was bitter. This bitterness affected both their views on the Security Treaty and President Eisenhower's visit. As a *Yomiuri* columnist said on May 19:

> They [cold war advocates in the U. S. and U.S.S.R.] will become all the more enthusiastic to have the Security Treaty

passed through the Diet. . . . A thaw in the cold war is a stream of history. Even those irresponsible people in the U. S. and U.S.S.R. who trampled on the spirit of Camp David will be unable to stem this stream.

Another general factor to be considered is the almost overwhelming sense of dissatisfaction in Japan today. The family unit upon which the Confucian system is based is passing, and the sense of totality once found in the emperor and the Establishment of the *ancien régime* is lost to the young. In its place are individual rights, but a right is license unless paired with responsibility. In Japan the confusion of individual freedom with irresponsibility is aggravated because individual rights were not personally acquired but directed from above during the Occupation. Thus, in one way the demonstrations and excesses of the spring of 1960 can be viewed as part of the experience needed to bring balance to freedom. Especially for the young, to whom one must look in a country where the ideas of the old are dead, the process of learning to think and act independently is difficult. The only immediate alternatives to a sudden rejection of the past are a yearning for the future or a recognition of the inadequacies of the present. The Japanese are too aware of time's passage to live in the future; and, as a result, their discontent with what one of their novelists has called "a transitional period in morality" is profound.

This discontent makes a large part of youth tend towards conscientious hedonism and another, smaller part, prone to abandon and violence. Another important group—the liberal intellectuals of the older generation—display the compulsive need to compensate for a failure of will during the era of the national cult. Their guilt feelings are directed especially towards the Right wing and the police, whom they once allowed to triumph, and towards China, the main house of Oriental culture against which they sinned.[7]

Thus dissatisfaction with the existing order—the "transitional period of morality"—plays an important part in any question involving large numbers of Japanese.

---

[7] China's position is unique. The feelings of guilt that came out of the war do not extend to any Western country or, for example, to Korea or the Philippines.

The above is a reproduction of the front page of the *Asahi* of June 17, 1960. The white-on-black headline above President Eisenhower's picture announces the "postponement" of his visit to Japan. The large box to the left of the picture of Prime Minister Kishi contains the joint statement against violence of the "Big Three" dailies in which they were joined by four other metropolitan newspapers.

The "Crusaders"   *Cartoon by Wu Yun*

Witnesses at the Signing Ceremony   *Cartoon by Mi Ku*

These two cartoons appeared in successive issues of the English language *Peking Review,* a weekly propaganda organ of the Chinese Communist regime. The cartoon by Wu Yun appeared in the January 19, 1960 issue and the cartoon by Mi Ku in the January 26, 1960 issue. They constitute representative samples of the materials used in the Chinese Communist propaganda campaign linking anti-Kishi, anti-American, and anti-Treaty themes.

The First Untruth

The first massive demonstration against the Treaty took place November 27, 1959, when the People's Council Against Revision of the Security Treaty [8] organized a nationwide "united action." At the Diet, where the main demonstration was held, 12,000 unionists and Zengakuren [9] students, the students in the lead, demonstrated in the Diet compound as well as in the streets surrounding the Diet. When the students had opened the gates into the compound late in the afternoon, there was no interference from the squads of police around the Diet yard nor were there any clashes with the police later. Sohyo Secretary-General Akira Iwai, who controlled the sound truck for the demonstration, allowed the truck to be driven into the compound where there were speeches for about an hour. Just after sunset the truck and most of the unionists left and the only scuffle of the day developed— between extremist Zengakuren students who wanted the truck to remain and the more moderate union leaders who wanted the demonstrators to disperse.

The following morning the three papers gave extensive coverage to the demonstrations, particularly to the fact that Socialist Party Secretary-General Asanuma had been in the Tokyo demonstration. The fact that the leader of the Opposition Party took part in a movement in front of the Diet was later widely exploited by the Government. The curious point, however, is that each of the national papers reported that Asanuma led the demonstrators into the Diet compound, in general making it appear his role had been vital. In fact Asanuma was little more than a spectator and entered the compound with other onlookers (including the writer) well after the demonstrators were inside. The *Asahi* and *Mainichi* reported the opposite, and the *Yomiuri* went further and provided a sensational account of Asanuma's daring.

The reporters who covered the story either substituted their hopes for the facts, because they would have liked Asanuma to

---

[8] The united front opposing the Treaty. The Socialist Party and Sohyo were its nucleus. The Japan Communist Party was not a member but acted as an "observer" in its councils.

[9] The Federation of Self-Governing Student Associations. It claims about 300,000 members (there are about 650,000 college students in Japan), but most of the members are uninterested in political affairs. The active cadres of Zengakuren are small, militant, and self-perpetuating. They are violently Leftist but, for the most part, not controlled by the Communists.

have taken the lead, or simply dramatized the event by choosing the most prominent person present to play the leading role. In any case, the Government Party was eager to believe it and the Socialists, as the "popular" party, were shy to deny it. When Asanuma was assassinated less than a year later it was as the victim of forces he himself had helped foster, by refusing to disclaim them, as early as the November 27 demonstration.

The national papers, like the Socialist Party, consider themselves "popular" and "progressive." Their reporting of Asanuma's role on November 27 is significant because it shows that long before the troubles of May and June of 1960, either through calculation or emotion, their coverage was sometimes distorted as they became captives of their own "popular" image. Their editorials were also distorted, not necessarily weighted towards the Opposition but necessarily weighted away from the Government and, in particular, away from Prime Minister Kishi.

It is important to note that the coverage was *sometimes* distorted. Few newspapers in the world are always consistent; correspondents in the field differ with each other in their judgments, and editors in the main office may differ with the correspondents. In the case of the national papers in Japan the coverage generally fluctuates on specific subjects that have a high degree of political sensitivity, such as the actions of the police. On these subjects the objectivity varied not only among the three papers day to day but often in an individual newspaper from day to day. Sometimes it would be weighted, sometimes objective. Editorial opinion followed the same devious windings, perhaps for two reasons: the "non-partisan" principle the press adheres to, which often amounts to expediency; and the lack of direct control from newspaper management, which makes a given policy impossible and allows the combination of reporters, desk supervisors, and copy editors who put out a certain edition to determine a large part of that edition's character.

In January 1960 Prime Minister Kishi flew to Washington to sign the Treaty. The day he left 700 Zengakuren students rioted at Haneda Airport, but for several months thereafter the Treaty issue was not of nationwide interest. During February, March, and April, the Diet deliberated on the Treaty. The People's Council staged various demonstrations and other maneuvers without receiving much support from other than the organized Left. Then on May 19 the Government Party forced a vote on the Treaty and the nature of the Treaty struggle overnight intensified dramatically and changed. The national newspapers were an important part of the events that followed.

In the following pages we examine their role in four sections: their coverage of the ratifying vote on the Treaty; their campaign against Kishi and the conservative Government; their partial support of the Opposition and their implicit support of the demonstrations; and lastly, their treatment of President Eisenhower's scheduled visit and the anti-American sentiment that had grown up around it.

The following is a listing of the sequence of events around which the role of the "big three" will be examined:

May 19, 1960—Diet Session Extended 50 days; Treaty Bill voted through Lower House.

May 26, 1960—Nationwide "United Action" against Kishi Government and Treaty.

June 4, 1960—Nationwide "United Action" and General Strike.

June 10, 1960—Attack on James Hagerty at Haneda Airport, Tokyo.

June 15, 1960—Nationwide "United Action"; Diet riot in which student was killed.

June 17, 1960—Cancellation of President Eisenhower's visit.

June 19, 1960—Proposed date of Eisenhower's arrival; Treaty automatically approved by Diet.

IV. THE FORCED VOTE
IN THE DIET

As deliberations on the Security Treaty drew to a close in May 1960, the three national newspapers emphasized their opposition to an early Diet vote on the Treaty, the position also taken by the Opposition Parties and, for different reasons, several dissident factions of the Liberal-Democrats. The *Asahi's* opposition to an early vote was based on a fundamental dissatisfaction with the Treaty; in a May 5 editorial it said it still believed economic and "political" bonds should replace military ties with the U. S. But in any case it favored, along with the *Yomiuri* and *Mainichi*, a national election prior to a Diet vote on the Treaty in order to test the public will.

All three papers pointed out that opposing views on the Treaty had not yet been "adjusted." An article in the May 13 *Yomiuri* stressed that the Miki-Matsumura and Kono factions of the Liberal-Democratic Party wanted the Diet session extended for two months to prevent a violent clash over the Treaty. The *Mainichi* in an editorial May 17 asked for dissolution of the Diet. The same day a roundtable discussion by reporters of the *Asahi* concluded that if parliamentarianism were to be protected (that is, if the Treaty were to be dealt with through "adjustment") the Treaty bill should not be passed "at a stroke."

On May 19, Prime Minister Kishi got the Treaty bill out of committee, opened a plenary session of the Diet, and forced votes on a fifty-day extension of the Diet and the Treaty bill, all within about eight hours.

The strategem evidently came as a surprise to most politicians; it was certainly a surprise to the public and apparently to the press. The pro-Government *Japan Times*, an English-language newspaper, reported that most Liberal-Democrats thought only an extension of the Diet would be taken up at the special night session. According to the *Japan Times*, "with the exception of a handful of top executives of the Party, the Tory Dietmen have not been told that the [Treaty] bill would be taken up at the session." The *Asahi* went further and reported in a May 22 article that "it is said that he [Speaker of the Lower House Ichiro Kiyose] decided to call policemen into the Diet without conferring with any other person beforehand."

The three national newspapers reacted violently; they were distressed by the suddenness of the maneuver and outraged that police had been used in the Diet building to expel Socialist members. The Socialists had themselves used force in an attempt to block the opening of the plenary session, a provocation, according to the Government, that justified the use of police. This reasoning, however, was not accepted by the bulk of the press, including the "big three."

Each paper devoted a large amount of space in its May 20 morning edition to the hectic eight hours that had ended shortly after midnight. On Page 1 there were banner headlines, pictures, and long articles. About half of an inside page was also given to pictures, mostly scenes of policemen grappling with Socialists. In addition each paper carried a story and pictures on Page 11 (later to become the page where the daily demonstrations were reported) specifically on the intervention of the police. The edition is of great significance, for in several ways it established the approach each of the three papers was to take during the next month in its reporting. For this reason sections of the lead stories on the vote and the special stories on police intervention have been translated in full and included as Appendix I.

May 20 Morning Editions

Among the three papers the coverage was uneven. All three more or less weighted their stories to win sympathy for the Socialists and make a villain of the Government, the *Asahi* more and the *Mainichi* and *Yomiuri* less.

The *Asahi* in its news articles used many expressions of emotion and value; of the three its reporting was the most subjective. Frequently it editorialized, describing the Treaty as being "passed wholesale," referring to the "job entrusted" to the "terrible police," and saying "the Liberal-Democrats used the police as a tool." According to the *Asahi* there were "spirited cries" from the Socialists while the Socialists were heckled "in a despicable way" by the Liberal-Democrats. In the special story on police intervention the *Asahi* used a rather jumbled colorific metaphor to propagandize against the Government: the "red" carpet of the Diet was "trampled on" by "policemen dressed in gray"; the "white roses" of peace which the Socialists wore in their lapels were "trampled into the red carpet," thus symbolizing "the way the authority of the Diet had been smeared with mud." The police wore "white gloves," but that could not absolve them from "the disgusting stain" they left on the Diet.

There was no clear exposition in the *Asahi* of the reasons why the police were brought into the Diet (the use of force by the Socialists being largely overlooked), nor was there any mention that the Socialists had been warned by the Speaker of the House before the police were called in. The impression remained, therefore, that the police had suddenly swooped in upon the Socialists after the police had first "silently climbed onto the red carpet of the Diet." The *Asahi* also outdid the *Mainichi* and *Yomiuri* by carrying a prominent article on the police on Page 1 (see Appendix I), in addition to the articles all three papers carried on Page 11.

In contrast to the *Mainichi* and *Yomiuri*, the *Asahi* underplayed the demonstration by Sohyo unionists and Zengakuren students that was being held outside the Diet at the time. Both the *Mainichi* and *Yomiuri* carried the demonstration story prominently on Page 1, the *Mainichi* quoting the People's Council for its figure of 25,-000 participants, the *Yomiuri* using the police count of 7,000.[1] The *Asahi* did not run its demonstration story on Page 1, but instead carried it on Page 11 without giving any numbers.

---

[1] But the *Yomiuri* in its Page 11 story said there were 30,000 participants in the demonstration. In all three papers throughout the Treaty struggle, the facts were more extraordinary and the writing more tendentious on Page 11 than on the front pages.

The *Mainichi* was the only paper to give a clear synopsis of the events during the afternoon and evening of May 19. In particular it pointed out that the Speaker of the Lower House had warned the Socialist Diet members about their use of force over an hour before the police were finally brought in. Like the *Asahi* its Page 11 story on the police was highly dramatic, but unlike the *Asahi* the situations "inside and outside" the Diet were featured together, thus roughly equating the pressures of the demonstrators outside the Diet with those of the police inside.

The *Yomiuri,* as usual, concentrated more on what it considered the highlights of the event. Its Page 1 story emphasized the "amazing confusion" in the Diet. The Page 11 story on the police was not especially dramatic for the *Yomiuri,* which is less concerned with dispassionate reporting than the other two papers. Mention was made of the warning given the Socialists, although it made it seem the police appeared rather more suddenly than they did.

May 20 Evening Editions

The press had been too surprised by the Government Party's action late on the night of May 19 to begin an editorial attack in earnest the next morning. The *Yomiuri* criticized the Liberal-Democrats for their coup, but at the same time found fault with the Socialists' use of force. The *Mainichi* criticized the Socialists less; and the *Asahi,* while calling the manner of the vote "undemocratic" and "unallowable," made no mention of the Socialists. By the evening of May 20, however, columnists were recovering from their shock. The *Asahi,* referring to the Socialist claim that 10 million people had signed petitions against the Treaty, said that some device would have to be found to make the Diet conform with the will of the people if the Government continued to refuse to dissolve the Diet. It offered a referendum as one possibility. The *Yomiuri* found the Diet vote "not fascistic, but fascism itself." It said Socialist tactics were a "problem," but considered them a legitimate "defense" against the Government Party's "attack" on free discussion.

The treatment of two smaller affairs in the evening editions of May 20 is also of interest. The injury the Speaker of the House received while trying to escape the Socialist seige of his office (requiring a month's hospitalization) was featured prominently on

Page 1 of the *Mainichi*. The *Yomiuri* published a story about half as large as the *Mainichi's*, giving the Speaker's views on the vote, but it did not mention his injury. The *Asahi* gave the injury small play—four lines on Page 1.

Foreign Minister Fujiyama's statement earlier that day that between 70 and 80 per cent of the country supported passage of the Treaty was given sizable space by the *Asahi* on Page 1, a smaller story by the *Mainichi*, and none at all by the *Yomiuri*.

Foreign commentary on May 20, was limited to Washington and Peking statements in the *Asahi* and the *Mainichi*. Both carried dispatches side by side on Page 2. Both also featured the Washington commentary more prominently, although the *Asahi's* story on Peking reaction was three times longer than the *Mainichi's*. The *Yomiuri* ignored Peking, and carried its Washington dispatch on Page 1. It also ran a Moscow interpretation on Page 2.

May 21 Morning Editions

The following morning editorials detailed the reactions of the press to the sudden Diet vote. The *Asahi* ran its long editorial on Page 1, which is highly unusual, describing the manner of the vote as "most evil" and the political situation as "fearful." It said the Diet was not a place where each side should try to win at all costs and criticized the Socialists for the senseless questions they had raised during deliberations on the Treaty. It said the Socialists often seemed to resist only "for their own sake," but that it had also become a habit in recent months for the Government Party to ignore the queries of the parliamentary Opposition—a "tyranny of the majority." It criticized the physical force resorted to by the Socialists as well as the "totalitarianism" existing in both parties. But since the ultimate responsibility for the forced vote and the introduction of police into the Diet belonged to the Government Party, it demanded that the Cabinet resign and the Diet be dissolved. The editorial said the nation had come "to the crossroads of parliamentary democracy, one road leading to its life, the other to its murder."

In addition to the special editorial the *Asahi* carried on Page 1 a lengthy article on criticism of Kishi within the Liberal-Democratic Party and a column castigating Kishi and calling for his resignation. On the second page much space was given to the Opposition

Parties' and Sohyo's demands for Kishi's resignation. Also on Page 1 was a cartoon showing the Diet building being "uprooted," the same idiomatic expression being used as had been used to describe the "uprooting" of the Socialists by the police.[2]

The *Mainichi* carried a large article on the differences between Kishi and the Kono and Miki-Matsumura factions in his own party. Its editorial was entitled, "It's All Kishi's Responsibility." It said that "Kishi's action has aggravated the opposition to him," but like the *Asahi* it found fault with the Opposition as well. It said that neither side had won nor lost, and that both the Opposition and the Government "used only words" in their debates and disregarded facts. As in the *Asahi*, the danger to parliamentary government was stressed: "We fear the evil influence of reverting to the ways of the past—the use of police and unilateral voting. The nation's trust in parliamentarian politics has been shaken." The *Mainichi* emphasized that this should be the first thing to be considered in regards to the events of May 19:

> The refusal of the Socialists to deliberate is also a problem, but it is a minor one compared to the Liberal-Democratic Party's and Government's plan to use force . . . the Kishi Cabinet, boasting of its victory, takes no notice of the voices calling for Diet dissolution.

The editorial said the paper was "deeply anxious" over the Opposition's tactics in the future.

> Our great fear is that the anti-Treaty forces will use the Government Party's tactics as an excuse to go beyond the law. If this should happen the great hopes for internal peace will be destroyed, and the crime would be the Kishi Cabinet's, because Kishi refuses to compromise.

Perhaps more than the *Asahi*, the *Mainichi* outlined what it thought should be done to overcome the threat to parliamentary democracy which both papers saw as a result of the May 19 events:

> We must attack both the Kishi Cabinet's use of force and the acts of those opposing the Treaty that undermine our law and order. . . . The fact that the opposition grows more virulent cannot be helped [because of Kishi's refusal to compromise]. But we must all calmly uphold law and order.

---

[2] Later a similar cartoon would show Zengakuren students pulling down the gate in front of Kishi's residence. The *Asahi* condemned the Zengakuren action when it took place, but with the feeling it was an inevitable (and therefore "logical") consequence of the original "uprooting."

The *Yomiuri* featured an article on Kishi's increasing estrangement in the political world, saying that he was being "isolated." Its editorial called the forced vote a rejection of democracy and an "invitation to fascism or a Leftist dictatorship." It said the Treaty had the "formality" but not the "essence" of approval, for "since the Treaty was ratified in this way, what kind of authority does it have?" The editorial criticized both sides for what had happened—the minority for its often irresponsible opposition, the majority for acting as if Japan were a one-party state—and warned about the future. "This kind of behavior within the Diet invites violence without." The *Yomiuri* also stressed that President Eisenhower's visit to Japan was now intimately involved with the Treaty, since it was passed exactly thirty days before the day of Eisenhower's scheduled arrival. (Under Japanese law a bill passed by the Lower House, if the Diet remains in session, becomes effective in thirty days automatically whether or not the Upper House acts upon it.)

The possibility of a forced vote on May 19, timed so that the Treaty would be automatically ratified on the day of Eisenhower's arrival, had been briefly mentioned before in unrelated articles in the press. Yet despite the apparent advantage of the tactic to the Kishi Government (and to the extreme Left), the press as well as the Opposition seemed slow to consider this aspect of the forced vote which later made it possible for anti-Kishi sentiment to be redirected against Eisenhower's visit. The *Yomiuri* was the exception. Perhaps because it is more sensitive to anti-Americanism than the other two papers, it was the first to comment editorially on the relevancy of Kishi's timing of the vote.[3]

Columns in the May 21 morning editions dealt with the dangerous consequences of a forced vote, all three calling for Kishi's resignation.[4] The *Yomiuri* column concentrated on the loss of international

---

[3] In the first days after the vote the *Asahi* mentioned its timing neither in news articles nor in editorials. The *Mainichi*, the day after the vote, mentioned the significance of the timing in its lead story, but subsequently it let the fact lapse. The *Yomiuri*, the same day as the *Mainichi*, hinted it had seen the vote coming, and, the next day, followed it up by discussing in an editorial Kishi's involvement of Eisenhower.

[4] Each of the three papers runs a daily column on Page 1 of its morning editions. They are unsigned, editorial-type commentary on almost any subject. Generally they are less formal, less pedantic, and less cumbersome than editorials. They give the reader an easy-to-digest opinion on some current topic and are extremely popular. They are better read and probably help form public opinion more than editorials. Although editorials are heavy pieces with large blocks of background material, they are, nonetheless, surprisingly well-read. Yet they generally end with weightless arguments calling for "self-reflection" or "sincerity," yawning cliches that never seem to tire Japanese who are engaged

prestige that would result from the use of police in the country's parliament. It called the use of police an act of "a fourth or fifth-rate power" and said it was "embarrassed that we have this kind of Prime Minister." The *Mainichi* column called the Diet vote an "arbitrary decision" and an "insolent act" because "the purpose of the [Diet] extension was not to make way for serious deliberations." It said the "people were made fools of" and that "doubts and uneasiness remain among the people." As for the dangers facing Japan, it felt there was

> no danger of [military] attack on Japan at the moment. The thing that has become dangerous is Kishi's political power. In order to satisfy his lust for power he has even sacrificed democracy. "Perhaps the methods were not appropriate, but the decision is still effective"—that is the excuse given. . . . Kishi's act of violence did the nation a dishonor in its attempt to make a decision on the Treaty.

Communist reaction to the passage of the Treaty was also carried on the morning of May 21. The *Mainichi* in a sizable Page 1 article quoted Peking, saying that 1,200,000 people had demonstrated spontaneously there against the Treaty. The *Asahi* carried adverse Peking and Moscow comment on the Treaty on Page 2 but made no mention of Peking's "spontaneous" demonstration. The *Yomiuri* carried no Communist reaction whatsoever.

A smaller story is also of interest. Undersecretary of State Douglas Dillon had issued a statement on May 20, that passage of the Treaty was of great importance to peace and security in the Far East. The *Mainichi* published this story on Page 1 in both its morning and evening editions of May 21; the *Yomiuri* published it on Page 1 of its morning edition only. The *Asahi* did not carry the story.

In the evening editions of May 21 the biggest stories in the *Mainichi* and *Yomiuri* were on a diplomatic note issued in Moscow May 20 warning the Japanese against providing bases for U-2's. It was the first major story from Moscow since the Diet vote on the Treaty, and both newspapers gave it large plays on Page 1 with four-column headlines, the *Yomiuri* using it as its lead story and the *Mainichi* as its second lead. The *Asahi,* on the other hand,

---

in being thoughtful. The regular Page 1 columns, therefore, are more in-fluential since they generally have a point to make and get on to it. Sometimes only one man writes the column, as in the case of the *Asahi,* and sometimes it may be done alternately by various members of the paper's editorial staff.

gave the Soviet warning a small story at the bottom of Page 1 with a one-column headline.

Characteristics

News coverage of the Treaty vote in the Lower House emphasized above all the introduction of police into the Diet building to expel a minority party. In any country this would be an ugly event, and in Japan, where the public is extremely sensitive to the political use of police, the press reacted with an emotional display. The *Asahi* in particular allowed emotionalism to distort its coverage, the *Mainichi* and the *Yomiuri* less so. The *Asahi*'s description of events made little attempt at objectivity, and unlike the *Mainichi* and the *Yomiuri*, gave a picture of Socialists pitted against police rather than Opposition Party pitted against Government Party.

It is immediately apparent that the selection of news articles as well as the emphasis given them varies not only from paper to paper but often within each paper day to day. Thus the Fujiyama statement favoring the Treaty was given a good play in both the *Asahi* and *Mainichi* and not run in the *Yomiuri*; while the Dillon statement favoring the Treaty was carried twice by the *Mainichi*, once by the *Yomiuri*, and not at all by the *Asahi*. The *Asahi* gave more space to Chinese Communist reaction one time than did the *Mainichi*, but in another edition it cut out the extreme propaganda statements from Peking which the *Mainichi* carried. The *Yomiuri* featured the Moscow warning, as did the *Mainichi*, but the *Asahi* underplayed it. Yet the *Yomiuri* ignored Peking comment both times it was run in the other papers. This inconsistency shows there is lack of overall control on the direction news coverage will take.

Editorially the general reaction of the three papers is well summed up by a *Mainichi* column in the morning edition of May 22. The column says that despite the obstructionist tactics of the Socialists, the police should not have been used in the Diet since the ends cannot justify the means.

> No matter how much the Treaty may serve Japan, it cannot be had by sacrificing democracy. . . . Democracy is the greater end.

It is noteworthy that interest in the Treaty itself was replaced by questions of how best to conduct parliamentary democracy.

Thus an *Asahi* column on the evening of May 21 criticized equally and severely the United States and the Communist camp for their "selfish" reactions to the passage of the Treaty. Both sides, it said, were "looking to their own ends" at the expense of Japanese democracy, thus making Japan "a ravine in the cold war." Serious discussion in the press turned from the advantages and disadvantages of the Treaty to "the greater end" of Japanese parliamentary democracy. The Treaty ceased to be in direct contention. Instead, the methods used by Kishi to secure the Diet vote made the Prime Minister himself the central issue in the press after May 19.

Yet again there is a curious inconsistency, this time in editorial reasoning. For although "the fact that the opposition grows more virulent cannot be helped . . . we must all calmly uphold law and order." In other words, the press, despite itself, already viewed certain future acts of the Opposition as inevitable if Kishi did not resign.

V. THE CAMPAIGN
AGAINST KISHI

Prior to the Vote

The campaign in the press against Prime Minister Kishi began long before his May 19 coup in the Diet, perhaps on the day he became Prime Minister. Ideologically the three national papers differed with Kishi. In general they were various degrees to the Left of Kishi's Right-of-Center Government. Their campaign against Kishi, however, did not continue to grow on intellectual content alone. In Japan, where emotion is predominant, ideological conviction can seldom provide the motive for an extended struggle; and the struggle in the press against Kishi lasted nearly two years.

The attacks began in earnest with Kishi's efforts to strengthen the powers of the police, a measure unpopular with much of the public and vehemently opposed by the Left. Kishi's effort failed in early 1959. In early 1960, revision of the Security Treaty had become the major issue, and a renewed attack began on the manner in which Kishi conducted Diet deliberations on the bill. But by that time it seemed as if getting Kishi out of power had become an *idée fixe* to the press. For nearly a year and a half he had been severely criticized. There was not much new for the press to say; they had to express their discontent by repeating the same charges over and over again. As they did Kishi became a symbol, to them and others, of all the faults of their democracy. Unknowingly perhaps, the image was becoming obsessional.

At the same time Kishi did little, if anything, to assuage the passions of the press. The *Times* of London referred to his missteps, rather gently, as "maladroit behavior." An example might be a statement he made in Hawaii in January 1960, to the effect that Japanese newspapers were so uninformative he never read anything but their sports pages. The three national papers pride themselves, and rightly so, on their international political coverage. They devote more space to items of high international news value than all but a handful of dailies in the United States, which is doubly remarkable considering they are mass circulation papers in a country without great influence internationally. Furthermore, Kishi's statement came when Diet deliberations on the Treaty were immediately ahead, a time when he could least afford to aggravate further the hostility of the press. Of course the press reacted to his "sports page" statement as might be expected.

In the Diet deliberations that began after Kishi returned from signing the Treaty in Washington in January, the Minority Parties took a position of extreme opposition. The press supported this "exhaustive questioning," although often it amounted to weeks spent on such matters as defining the "Far East." [1] The Government was not prepared for such details, or minutiae, and the size of the Far East fluctuated daily; by February 26, the term had been so abused by the Socialists, the Government contracted it to include only the area "north of the Philippines where territories are under the Republic of Korea or Chinese Nationalist rule." It was obvious the Opposition was dallying, but the press pounced on Kishi's Government for its inability to answer questions on the Treaty directly.

A more substantial issue exploited by the Opposition—whether the "prior consultation" clause in the Treaty gave Japan de facto veto power over the dispatch of U.S. military units from Japan to other areas—was also handled ineptly by the Government, raising more doubts in editorials.

The interpellations were covered at great length in the press, but in general the debates seemed obtuse. The national papers found fault with the irrelevancy of some arguments raised by the

---

[1] The area delimited by the Treaty. The preamble to the Treaty states that Japan and the U.S. have a "common concern in the maintenance of international peace and security in the Far East," and Article IV states that they shall "consult together . . . whenever the security of Japan or international peace and security in the Far East is threatened." The Socialists did not want the "Far East" to be defined to include Communist China and the countries on its land borders.

Opposition, while at the same time growing more angry at Kishi's "evasive and wily answers." Both Government and Opposition seemed unwilling or unable to debate the Treaty meaningfully or decisively. The national papers felt the frustration of this, but again it was Kishi's obscurantism that they found almost entirely to blame. Exhaustive (and often irrelevant) questioning was a shrewd tactic for the Socialists since they had no other way to combat the Government Party's absolute majority. The press in general accepted the Socialists' arguments, thinking this sort of questioning was necessary for "full debate." Kishi himself had difficulty making the case for the Treaty clear, which was complicated by the uneven support he received from the various factions of his own party.

As the deliberations droned on, columnists began to intersperse discussions of the Treaty with attacks on Kishi, so that the two gradually became synonomous. Political affairs in Japan often degenerate into personal causes, and the impression was growing in the press during the spring of 1960 that the Treaty was intimately connected with Kishi's own personal interests. Kishi himself was either guilty of this or unable to recognize its possible consequences. In any case, he made no effort to counter the allegations. By May, the lack of progress in the deliberations had dismayed the national dailies and convinced them their suspicions about Kishi were true. The *Yomiuri* said flatly in a May 6 editorial that it was obvious Kishi was trying "to perpetuate his regime on the basis of the new Security Treaty." The failure of the summit meeting in Paris was also a factor. A column in the *Yomiuri* of May 17 drew a parallel to a small kingdom that had survived in ancient China between two more powerful neighbors. Rather than adopt the Treaty, the column said, Japan should maneuver skillfully between "King Khrushchev and King Ike." [2]

---

[2] The *Yomiuri* columnist discusses the Treaty as if it were an internal affair only and as if Japan were not a part of the present world scene. As happened so often during the Treaty struggle, the press ignored the actual international position of Japan. In world trade, Japan's bread and butter, Japan sells more to the U. S. than to any other country; and, next to Canada, Japan is the best customer of the U. S. abroad. Over a billion dollars worth of trade is exchanged each way, about twenty times the amount exchanged with the U.S.S.R.

Even if the enormous cultural and social effects of the U. S. on Japan (and the lack of them by the U.S.S.R) are disregarded, the economic relations between the two countries make the *Yomiuri* analogy wistful and specious to anyone but a doctrinaire neutralist of the Left.

After the Vote

After the Treaty was forced through the Lower House, the three national papers attacked Kishi daily and demanded he take "responsibility" for what had happened. The *Mainichi* in an editorial May 22 said parliamentarianism had been "trampled upon" and that "confidence in Kishi has completely disappeared." A *Yomiuri* column the same day said Kishi was used to saying "protect democracy and parliamentarianism, but, these words [for him] have no content; they are only slogans." The next day an *Asahi* column said that "Kishi thinks not of Japan's fate but of the fate of the Kishi Cabinet," and the *Yomiuri* column, criticizing Kishi's statement that the press did not represent the public, said that "in doing this he has clearly displayed the face of a dictator." The *Mainichi*'s column May 24 expanded the attack to say that Secretary-General Kawashima of the Liberal-Democratic Party "thinks like a dictator"; on May 25 it criticized Kishi for being "uncooperative" towards the press; on May 26 it said Kishi "is now standing at a vital crossroads, one road leading to dictatorship; if he resigns Japan's politics and he himself may be saved."

The press also freely drew parallels between the situation in Japan and those in South Korea and Turkey, whose regimes had recently been overthrown by violence.[3] The *Mainichi* said in an editorial May 22: "When we look at the result of the Rhee incident, we cannot be patient. In order for such an unfortunate thing not to happen here, the Kishi Cabinet should resign immediately." An *Asahi* column on May 28 said "it is also worthy of note" that the ruling parties in South Korea and Turkey had had absolute majorities, and that "the direct cause of the overthrow of the Menderes regime was its ignorance of parliamentarianism." A *Yomiuri* column the same day, commenting on Turkey, said

> fortunately Japan has no military, nor a Privy Council. This, however, means there is nothing that will be able to control the Prime Minister's strength. Therefore Prime Minister Kishi is now having everything his own way. History proves, however, that in the end it is impossible for any ruler to defeat public opinion.

---

[3] Another example of the press hinting that violence might be the *inevitable* result if Kishi remained in power. The "logical" necessity of the Opposition's resorting to violence, though neither explained nor condoned outright, was implicitly assumed.

Also on May 28, the *Asahi* cartoon showed a student asking a Japanese soldier for help. The soldier was shaking his head, and, consonant with the hapless military spirit of postwar Japan, saying "No, I'm about to be discharged." The *Mainichi* carried a more serious cartoon that day, showing Kishi in a rowboat with two haggard fishermen. Kishi was saying, "Korea was No. 1, Turkey was No. 2, No. 3?" Finally, however, in an editorial May 30 the *Mainichi* admitted Turkey and South Korea were "stones from a different mountain."

"Public Opinion"

Perhaps nothing infuriated the press more than Kishi's statement that the newspapers did not represent public opinion. The *Asahi's* column May 24, in reference to the barbed wire that had been placed around Kishi's residence after continual assaults by Zengakuren students, said, "if he thinks he can defend himself from public opinion by wire entanglements, he is being naive." The statement is also interesting for the way it tacitly condones student violence in the name of "public opinion."

Editorials May 29, all concentrated on "public opinion" as represented by demonstrators. The *Yomiuri* was the mildest. It said those "demanding the resignation of the Kishi Cabinet are not just students and workers; they represent nothing less than the public opinion of one part of society." The *Asahi* reverted to the theme of ultimate responsibility: "It doesn't have to be said that violence is wrong. But since Prime Minister Kishi's politics have caused the demonstrations, to condemn them simply as violence is, we believe, an excuse." The *Mainichi* was similarly equivocal about the use of violence. It said it agreed "in principle" with Kishi that it would be wrong for him to resign because of extra-parliamentary pressures, but it went on to say that "we cannot accept a situation where the Prime Minister, whose party holds an absolute majority, will not listen to public opinion and will not resign until he has served his term no matter what happens." A *Mainichi* column the same day hinted at what might happen if Kishi did not resign:

> Kishi has decided everything that disagrees with his opinions is incorrect. . . . If Kishi falsely reads public opinion and continues to adhere to his self-righteous, unyielding position, it

would be impossible to say there is no danger of his inviting this most evil of situations [reference to Korea and Turkey].

The *Asahi* column May 30 said there was

> no precedent for the severity of criticism against the Government in newspapers all over the country. The great scale of the protest demonstrations is also unusual. Yet Kishi still says this is not public opinion.

The *Yomiuri,* in its column May 31 agreed that

> to bow to violence outside the Diet would set a bad precedent, but the "voiceless voices" outside the Diet are saying, "Kishi-san, by resigning please settle this confused political situation." The fact that these voices cannot be heard is bad.

The *Mainichi* column the same day, although pointing out that the situation in Japan was not the same as in South Korea or Turkey, emphasized that Rhee's false ideas on public opinion had been instrumental in making him "self-righteous and dictatorial."

The *Asahi's* column the morning of June 4, the day Sohyo held its illegal railroad strike, summarized the case the press had built for Kishi's ultimate responsibility. In an apologia for the illegal strike, the column noted that Kishi "had sown the seed of this confusion," and said Kishi's claim that the strike was "a denial of democracy . . . looks like the case of a monkey telling someone else, your bottom is red."

Public Opinion Polls

The personal criticism of Kishi was most extensive in the national dailies the first week after the Diet vote. Of the 20 cartoons printed in the three papers during that week 18 were political; 13 deprecated Kishi, four the Government Party, and one was directed against the police. In the *Mainichi* and the *Asahi* five out of the seven cartoons each paper ran were directed against Kishi, in the *Yomiuri* three out of six. During the rest of the month the political focus shifted somewhat. Of 13 cartoons ten were political: four on Eisenhower, two on Kishi, two on demonstrations, and two on strife within the Government Party. The editorial emphasis during this period before the demonstrations became massive is also revealing.

The *Asahi,* for example, between May 20 and June 3, ran four editorials on Kishi, three on the anti-democratic methods of the Government and Government Party, two on parliamentarianism, and *none* on the Treaty itself.

Various newspaper polls during the period were used to try to show the shift of public opinion away from the Treaty. A *Yomiuri* poll of October 4, 1959, found that 46 per cent of the public thought the Treaty necessary, 12 per cent unnecessary, and 42 per cent had no opinion. An *Asahi* poll of January 18, 1960, reported that 29 per cent of the public thought the Treaty desirable, 25 per cent undesirable, 6 per cent had other opinions, and 40 per cent had no opinions. The *Yomiuri* found on April 23, 1960, that 28 per cent thought the Treaty would be ratified, 21 per cent thought it would not, and 51 per cent had no opinions. The wording of the polls is significant, for necessity and desire do not always coincide. What the polls do show is that even towards the end of deliberations, after the Treaty had been featured in the press every day for months, over half the public still was so unconcerned it had no opinion on the Treaty's ratification.

The press attached great significance to a later poll taken after the Diet vote. Kishi had countered the campaign against him in the press, which was then at its peak, by saying that the "voiceless voices" of the nation supported him. The *Asahi* took a poll May 25 and 26 to attempt to disprove this and published the results June 2 and 3. The results of the poll were widely featured in the three national papers to prove that in fact, they, not Kishi, were representing the "voiceless voices" and the public as a whole.

According to the *Asahi* the poll was "national" and had queried 3,000 people in the "selective method".[4] The seven questions and their results published June 2 and the two published June 3 are all included because they made up the bulk of the newspapers' justifications that their campaign represented the "opinions of the voiceless voices."

---

[4] The *Asahi* itself conducted the poll, apparently without the aid of a professional, or objective, poll-taking agency. In publicizing the results of the poll the newspaper failed to explain either what a "national" poll was or how it went about selecting people under the "selective method." Yet despite these serious omissions and the fact that the *Asahi* was the most subjective in its news coverage of Kishi and the Treaty struggle, the poll was given a large replay by other newspapers and commentators.

1) Do you think the actions of the Government and the Liberal-Democratic Party (LDP) during deliberations on the Treaty were good?

    6% good
    50% bad
    18% neither good nor bad
    25% no answer
    1% other

2) Do you think the actions of the Socialist Party (SP) during deliberations on the Security Treaty were good?

    11% good
    32% bad
    31% neither good nor bad
    25% no answer
    1% other

3) Do you think the actions of the Democratic-Socialist Party (DSP) during deliberations on the Treaty were good?

    8% good
    13% bad
    43% neither good nor bad
    34% no answer
    2% other

4) According to the LDP, the LDP had to pass the Treaty unilaterally because the SP would never have let the Treaty come into existence if they could have done anything about it. Do you agree with that statement? Do you disagree?

    13% agree
    47% disagree
    34% no answer
    6% other

5) According to the SP and DSP, it was wrong for the LDP to pass the Treaty unreasonably and unilaterally because the regular Diet session had not yet expired. Do you agree with that statement? Do you disagree?

    45% agree
    16% disagree
    34% no answer
    5% other

6) It is said that "the methods of the Government and the LDP are bad" and it is also said that "the methods of the SP, or the DSP, are bad." Which do you agree with? (0 indicates very few answers, under 1%).

29% Gov't and LDP bad
8% SP bad
0% DSP bad
15% Gov't and all three parties bad
3% Gov't and LDP and SP bad
2% SP and DSP bad
0% All three parties bad
8% other
35% no answer

7) Do you think the present Diet as representatives of the people are actually working for the people? Do you think not?

17% working for the people
56% don't think so
5% other
22% no answer

1) Do you think the Kishi Cabinet is good?

	Good	Bad	Reason: Gov't's politics poor	Disregards public opinion, acts dictatorially	Time for a change
1957—July	40%	14%	6%	. . . .	. . . .
1957—Nov.	36%	19%	6%	. . . .	. . . .
1958—Sept.	34%	23%	13%	. . . .	. . . .
1959—Feb.	28%	34%	10%	. . . .	. . . .
1960—Jan.	33%	32%	11%	3%	2%
1960—May	17%	48%	6%	14%	4%

(24% no answer)
(11% other)

2) Would it be better to keep the Kishi Cabinet or would it be better to change it?

	keep it	change	other	no answer
1960—Jan.	28%	44%	6%	22%
1960—May	12%	58%	9%	21%

The first three questions showed only that the public was displeased with the way all the parties conducted Diet deliberations: 6 per cent said the Government Party's actions had been "good," 8 per cent said the Democratic-Socialists' had been, and 11 per cent said the Socialists'. The next two questions were more relevant, for they were the only ones in which nearly half of those queried made a positive statement on political methods. In both nearly half said they favored compromise in the Diet. The sixth and seventh questions were only useful in emphasizing the distrust and suspicion the average Japanese voter feels for politicians. In the sixth 50 per cent said they had no opinion or thought all the parties and the Government were "bad"; in the seventh 78 per cent said the Diet did not represent the people or that they had no opinion on it.

The first question in the second section is particularly interesting, for it shows that ideological discontent with the Treaty was very small. During this struggle between Government and Opposition, the press directed its argument not primarily against the Treaty bill itself, as it had done against the police bill the year before, but rather against Kishi. This was reflected in the poll, showing the effect the campaign in the press had had on the public. Of those who found the Kishi Cabinet "bad" at the time the police bill was the major issue (February 1959), nearly one-third had said their reason was the policies of the Government. (The other reasons were the traditional ones in Japanese politics: corruption, faction politics, no faith in the prime minister). In January 1960, when the Treaty was the major issue but before the press had begun its campaign against Kishi, approximately one-third still gave Government policies as their reason. But in May 1960, the figure had dropped to one-eighth; nearly one-third now considered Kishi's disregard for public opinion as their primary reason for disliking his Government, a reason that had not even appeared until the press began its campaign against Kishi in earnest. Subsequently its rise coincides with the newspapers' increasingly personal attacks on Kishi, especially after his "sports page" statement against the press and his "voiceless voices" accusation.

Of course the *Asahi* and the other papers that quoted the poll for self-justification read it differently. They interpreted it as showing only that Kishi was unpopular. The *Asahi* said in the article accompanying the poll on June 3:

> In various ways the poll shows just what support there is for the Kishi Cabinet, and whichever way the poll is looked at, the support is bad. It also shows that the voices calling for Kishi's resignation are increasing at various levels and intensities.

For the press this was a mandate to continue proving Kishi's personal culpability for the state of the nation, including the growing excesses of the Left.[5]

---

[5] In fact, the results of the poll, even though gathered by the *Asahi*, do not especially validate the *Asahi*'s contentions on public opinion. More than anything else they indicate an apathetic public, a large part of which was without opinion or disgusted with everyone.

VI. IN SUPPORT OF
THE DEMONSTRATIONS

Despite the vitriolic campaign against Kishi, the Socialists were held accountable for the share of overall "responsibility" the press believed was theirs. The unspoken creed of Japanese journalism did not mean the Opposition was right because the Government was wrong. Immediately after the forced vote, the official Socialist position—stated by Secretary-General Asanuma to the effect that the Government's use of force inside the Diet made the Opposition's future tactics inevitable—was attacked by all three national papers in their May 25 editorials. The *Mainichi* said the Socialist Party was using the same excuse the Government had, the one Japanese often lapse into to evade an issue: "it can't be helped."

This was followed by other warnings during the first week after the Diet vote. In its editorial, May 25, the *Mainichi* had said that "any mass movement should have its rules and bounds. What is most important for a mass movement is to achieve its objectives while not creating social unrest." [1] The following day the paper crit-

---

[1] While advocating "not creating social unrest," the press at the same time was helping to create it. The analogies of the Japanese Government to the recently overthrown Governments in Korea and Turkey, mentioned earlier, and the continual references to the "inevitability" of violence unless Kishi resigned, are examples. In fact what the press itself was doing and what it said should be done were two different things. Day after day the three national papers implied that violence was inevitable, yet when Asanuma said as much in plain words they all three criticized him. In their fervor to assign "responsibility" the national papers completely missed the irony of their own behavior.

[48]

icized Asanuma for going directly to the American Embassy to see
Ambassador MacArthur, and the *Asahi*, in an editorial warning to
the leaders of the Left, demanded that the nationwide demonstrations to be held that day be moderate. In an editorial, May 28, the
Asahi again called for self-restraint and, along with the other
two papers, criticized demonstrators for going to Kishi's and Foreign
Minister Fujiyama's private residences. It said "the Socialist Party
should feel responsible for recent excessive demonstrations, instead
of being pleased by them."

By June 8, the condemnation was more open. An *Asahi* editorial
that day, after the usual preface castigating Kishi, was almost as
harsh on the Socialists as it was on the Government. "It is perfectly
obvious the responsibility for adjusting the present situation be-
longs to the Government . . . but that does not mean anything
is permissible for the Opposition Party." This, the *Asahi* said, would
be

> the beginning of the end of parliamentarianism. . . . [If the
> country] is falling under the black shadow of fascism again as
> the Socialists claim, then they should return to the Diet rather
> than continue to help create a situation where there is one
> party in the Diet pitted against masses outside the Diet. . . .
> Is it [the Socialist attitude] a product of excitement, merely
> short-sightedness, or because their whole outlook is extraordi-
> narily simple-minded?

Following the attack on James Hagerty's car at Tokyo's Haneda
Airport June 10,[2] the *Asahi* faltered slightly and approached the
problem from the opposite side. An editorial, June 12, concerned
with the loss of public support to Sohyo that would result from the
"reckless violence," said it did not want unions to lose their "sensitivity to public opinion and the trends of middle-of-the-road
thought." The *Asahi* column that evening was less timid; it violently
criticized the Haneda disorder as well as the demonstrators who
had been using stones and paint and burning newspapers at Kishi's
residence. "The responsibility of demonstration leaders is indeed
heavy," it said. "The demonstration that ceases to be orderly becomes simply a mob, nothing more than a crowd of rioters."

The *Yomiuri's* editorial that same morning, disregarding Sohyo's
alleged sensitivity to what went on in the middle-of-the-road, made
up in vigor what the *Asahi* lacked. It said the Socialists should be

---

[2] Hagerty was coming to Tokyo to make final arrangements for President
Eisenhower's visit nine days later. The riot staged when he arrived and the
significance of the groups that participated in it will be discussed in the section
on Eisenhower's visit.

blamed for the attack on Hagerty's car because the participants were members of the People's Council, of which the Socialists supposedly were in charge. The following day, June 13, both its editorial and column were directed against the Socialists. The editorial said in part:

> The leadership of Sohyo and the People's Council Against the Security Treaty is confident it can control mass demonstrations, but already extreme Leftism is sprouting among those beneath them, as was shown in the violent events at Haneda Airport. Sohyo itself well knows what is at the heart of this—the influence of its militant action in disregarding the Public Workers Law and stopping the trains [in the June 4 general strike]. Before we fall into the violence of extreme Leftism, this dangerous bud must be torn out. Even though they [demonstrations] are called mass actions to defend democratic politics, they must not go beyond democratic politics. There is a limit.[3]

The *Yomiuri* column denounced the Socialists for refusing to compromise with the Government and for evading responsibility for the Haneda riot.

> Cannot the Socialist Party gradually become adult? It doesn't make any practical preparations for power; it only stands in the forefront of demonstrations saying *wassho, wassho* in absolute opposition. . . . Indeed, the fact is the Socialist Party often finds itself, like a child, heroically excited by its own strikes and demonstrations. Its behavior is that of some emotional political party in the era before the war—illegal and unproductive. It is by no means a thing of democracy. . . . It is losing the character of a leader of popular movements in a democratic, peaceful country. . . . During these many days we have lost patience with the childishness of the Socialist position of absolute opposition.

The *En Masse* Resignation

Another issue on which the national papers scored the Socialists was the party's proposed *en masse* resignation from the Diet. Although this plan to force the dissolution of the Diet was never tried, it was strongly advocated for several weeks by Sohyo and the

---

[3] The *Asahi* on the other hand, while going so far as to complain that a "demonstration that ceases to be orderly becomes simply a mob," carefully avoided any mention of "extreme Leftism" in its coverage of the attack on Hagerty.

extreme Left of the party. (Sanzo Nosaka, Secretary-General of the Communist Party, interestingly enough was one of those against it.) The *Mainichi* was the most outspoken against the Socialists, calling the resignation "anti-democratic" in a June 1 editorial and "about the same offense" as the Government's unilateral deliberations. In a column the following day the paper said that "at the very least the legality of the [Government's voting] procedure is strong. Not recognizing this would create a harmful precedent for the future." This was followed by a column June 3 and another editorial on the subject June 7:

> We also think there is no way to settle the present crisis except through the Cabinet's resignation and dissolution of the Diet; but we do not agree that an en masse resignation of Socialists from the Diet should be one of the means to achieve this end.

The *Yomiuri's* opinion was similar. In an editorial June 2 it said that "with this kind of final protest it is conceivable a change in the political situation could be speeded. However, to rectify the situation with this sort of pathetic action would be far too harmful an influence on parliamentarianism." It opposed the resignation again in a column, June 3, and added in one, June 7, that the Socialists would be rejecting their responsibilities to their electorate, which "cannot be called the way to act in a democracy." The *Asahi* criticized the Socialist plan in editorials, June 2 and 6.

A point brought out in the June 2 *Asahi* editorial was the case of the Social-Democrats of the Weimar Republic, who had "resigned in 1931" and "never appeared" again. This theme runs consistently through the newspaper commentary of the period, showing the press was particularly wary of Leftist excesses triggering a Rightist reaction, a "reversal into the opposite." The *Mainichi* warned in a column, May 25, that Zengakuren's violence was dangerous both in itself and because the Government could use it to conceal its "*coup d'état*," but it was the *Asahi* that most frequently discussed the parallel with pre-Nazi Germany.

It mentioned it in an editorial, May 22, before the demonstrations had begun to grow in size, and warned, like the *Mainichi*, that if the demonstrations grew excessive they could bring repressive legislation. Several weeks later, after the attack on Hagerty, the *Asahi's* editor-in-chief wrote a special commentary in his paper that ran in several parts. The editor was Shintaro Ryu, who a week later initiated the joint declaration against violence that was published in most major newspapers throughout the country. In his June 11 commentary after the Haneda riot he again warned that the use of force by the Opposition would lead to anti-democratic laws.

> We must recall the error of pre-war Germany and not repeat it. . . . To wield force without thinking of its consequences involves a serious risk.

Actually the *Asahi* did not have to look as far as the Weimar Republic for its precedent of danger. The rise in internationalist ideas in Japan's relatively liberal society of the 1920's was an important reason for the growth, in reaction, of ultranationalist societies in the 1930's. Today there is one significant difference: most of the xenophobists are on the extreme Left; so much so that the selfless, reckless provocateurs of Zengakuren strikingly resemble the junior officers of the prewar army. But despite this difference, the press was able to recognize the Japanese predilection for abrupt reaction, especially when racism is involved, and to warn of it.

Direct Action

On the issue of extra-parliamentary tactics the press equivocated in varying degrees, the *Asahi* and *Mainichi* more than the *Yomiuri*. Both of the two larger papers agreed direct action was fundamentally undemocratic, but at the same time they found excuses for tolerating it. In other words they reversed their tendency to treat relatives as absolutes, and, instead, this time treated an absolute as a relative. The *Mainichi* agreed with Kishi in a May 28 column that a prime minister could not resign because of extra-parliamentary pressure, "but in this case," it went on, "the demonstrations are only the organized followers of an opinion general among the public. . . . More and more people gradually are joining; in the streets people shake the hands of demonstrators as they pass." In an editorial, June 2, the paper was more explicit. It said that "in general it is true" that a democratically elected government should not surrender to direct action, "but if that is the case [Kishi] must decide what is to be done before the situation becomes grave and act to end the impasse."

Obviously there was only one thing Kishi could do to satisfy the press: resign, and thus in effect give credence to the efficacy of direct action. The *Asahi* in a column the same day went even further and resisted the idea that massive demonstrations in front of the Diet were a form of extra-parliamentary pressure: "Is not the nation 'outside' the Diet," it asked, "actually the 'inside' of the Diet?"

The *Yomiuri* accepted neither of these arguments, and, throughout the month following the forced vote, it grew increasingly intolerant of the Leftist rationalizations. The day after the vote, which it called an act of fascism, the *Yomiuri* column said that "from the standpoint of parliamentarianism, the Socialist Party should be censured for its violent tactics." On May 24 the paper's column said the Socialists would have to realize, "Japan is not so backward a country that its political course can be changed by demonstrations." An editorial, June 7, said that even though the general strike three days earlier had had wide public support, "it would be wrong for the Socialist Party to rely completely on movements outside the Diet . . . A crisis in parliamentary politics can be resolved only if all efforts center on the Diet itself." Its column the same day said that

> certainly there is no doubt Japan's democracy is seriously ill . . . . in order to protect democracy [Kishi] refuses to resign or dissolve the Diet, and the Socialists, in order to protect democracy, hold endless strikes and demonstrations to make Kishi resign and dissolve the Diet. It seems that both sides advocate a sanguinary way to destroy democracy in the name of democracy.

The three papers immediately after the forced vote began to justify demonstrations as a legitimate show of antagonism to the Government. Their attitudes varied, however, as the Socialist campaign gained momentum.

During the first week after the vote (May 20-26) they were generally apprehensive that demonstrations would be Leftist agitations without public support and therefore prone to grow extreme. This fear was reinforced May 20, when Zengakuren's Trotskyite wing attacked Kishi's private residence. The press severely condemned the action, but beyond that their feelings were ambiguous. The *Asahi* in an editorial May 22 attempted to differentiate between changing a political situation through mass movements, which it considered undemocratic, and demonstrations that were an "expression of the people's will" (and also might change the political situation), which it justified. The only apparent difference between the two was that allowable mass movements were those "carried out in an orderly manner without violence." In other words, the *Asahi's* position on extra-parliamentary pressure was opportunistic. It solved the dilemma of choosing direct action or democratic procedure by a relativist's answer that disregarded the question. Then, for those who might have thought events were so relative that 12th century principles were still in practice, the editorials also pointed out that the country was not split as it had been in the Genji-Heike era, and rather that the Government, Opposition, and people were all "in the same boat."

Two days later an *Asahi* editorial again criticized Zengakuren attacks on Kishi's residence, saying "[We] absolutely oppose . . . semiviolent" demonstrations. The editorial went on to say that "it is the mission of democratic politics, however, to prevent the emergence of conduct which calls forth such thoughtless action. High-handed politics gives rise to irregular counter-measures." The *Asahi* column the morning of May 26 also condemned Zengakuren's violence, but apparently more in order to prove the case for Kishi's resignation than because it thought violence was inherently evil. The column ended: "Kishi-san, you are being forsaken by the nation. You and your Cabinet step down. Then things will grow quiet." An *Asahi* editorial the next day also treated Zengakuren's violence as a tool to be used. "We, too, do not want demonstrations to assume violent proportions. It is essential to prevent such a situation. That is why we think Prime Minister Kishi should make up his mind [to resign] without delay." [4]

The *Asahi* was willing to accept the contradiction, to condemn violence, and at the same time add it to their arsenal. The *Mainichi* did so less, while the *Yomiuri*, even at that early date, was notably unsanguine in regards to popular demonstrations. In a column, May 26, it called snake dances, red flags, and *hachimaki* (headbands worn by demonstrators, traditionally by Japanese heroes for courage) "barbaric" in themselves and "a form of violence." It also punned on the inability of Japanese to transliterate Western words without confusing their meanings, noting sardonically that "democracy" in Japan seemed to mean nothing more than "living by demonstrations." ("Demokurashi" is the transliterated word for

---

[4] There are numerous examples of a newspaper developing in an editorial an idea that had first appeared in its Page 1 column a few days before. Since the Page 1 columns are more out-spoken and extreme than editorials, one wonders if this is a case of the tail wagging the dog. It shows that the front-page column is not only immensely influential among subscribers, but among the editors as well.

"democracy," but "demo" is also the Japanese word for "demon-strations", and "kurashi" means "living".)

The May 26 "United Action"

The next period lasted from May 26, the day of the first "united action" after the forced vote, to some time after June 4, the day of the general strike. This was the time when the press most vigorously supported the Opposition and its tactics. The support reached its peak June 4 and wavered until June 10, when the riot against Hagerty brought a new assessment. Newspaper propagandizing, both editorially and in news columns, was most severe during this period.

Several factors allayed the apprehensions the press had had immediately after the vote. First, the base of support for the Opposition (in Tokyo at least) grew daily; and second, the demonstrations, with the exception of those staged by Zengakuren's Trotskyite wing, were generally orderly. The second point, the press said, was proved by the calmness of the nationwide "united action" on May 26, the first point on May 24 when 600 *bunkajin* (men of culture) [5] demonstrated in front of the Diet. It was the

---

[5] *Bunkajin* literally means "man of culture," but its importance to the Japanese is more allusive. The function of the *bunkajin* is roughly equivalent to that of the "intellectual" in Western Europe, but the term is both more inclusive and less vague. "Culture" (*bunka*) itself is more general in meaning than the English word, and a *bunkajin* appears to be anyone who, by profession, communes with the historic Japanese spirit, the "culture" of the race. This excludes merchants, financiers, politicians, and others interested in money and non-spiritual power. It includes poets, professors, scientists, artists, actresses, pottery craftsmen, *go* masters, the makers of traditional Japanese musical instruments, and a host of other people who are concerned with what is considered the nation's unique sensibility.

Normally there are only two requirements for a *bunkajin:* that he not be engaged in business and that he excel. Once a person becomes a member of the *Bunka* Establishment he is entitled to comment on everything. For example, the opinion of a research scientist (especially if he is a nuclear scientist) may be solicited on an intricate political question and given wide play in the press, even though he obviously knows nothing about the subject. "Critics" (free-lance writers able to commune but unable to find a profession) are the only members of the *Bunka* Establishment who are not working culturists.

The term has more or less replaced the postwar *intelli* (intellectual), which had inapplicable Western overtones of logic, rationality, and knowledge, and was not able to describe the traits admired. During May and June, the *bunkajin* was always included in news articles if the paper was trying to show the demonstration had profound roots. Thus the *Asahi* in a Page 1 story, June 5, describing a demonstration that had been held at the American Embassy the day before, emphasized eloquently that it was made up of "workers, women, and *bunkajin*."

first time the *bunkajin* class had taken to the streets, and the national papers attached great significance to it. It was proof, they said, that the demonstrations were no longer the work of only the *organized* Left, but rather had developed a truly national character.

By May 26, it was common for news articles on demonstrations to begin with a stream of propaganda. The slogans were put in quotes, but nonetheless they invariably led off each article; for example: "Under the cries of 'down with Kishi', 'dissolve the Diet', 'block ratification of the Security Treaty', the national unified action. . . ."

In reporting the May 26 demonstrations held throughout the country, the *Asahi,* both in its main headline and lead story, described the demonstrators as irresistibly "rolling forth like a wave." Its description was dramatic, less poetic than on May 20 but just as breathless. The *Mainichi,* the morning of May 27, also called the demonstrators "a tidal wave", and emphasized they were made up of "workers from different regions, students, men of culture, and farmers." It reported for the first time in any of the three papers the new chant of "cancel Ike's visit," and said that such numbers "had never been seen before." An *Asahi* column the same morning pointed out that the demonstration had not included just workers and students but a wide cross-section of the citizenry.

The press, having decided the demonstrations were popular and national, did its best to report them in that light.[6]

The Police, the Right-wing and the American Embassy

It is recalled that the use of police in the Diet, May 19, had particularly appalled the press. Perhaps more than anything else it had caused the distorted coverage of the forced vote. This sensitivity toward the police influenced, though to a lesser extent, the reporting of the demonstrations that followed. In fact, whenever

---

[6] It is certainly true that the variety of groups participating in the demonstrations grew daily after the forced vote in the Diet. Such non-militants as a YMCA unit began to take part regularly. But although the *make-up* of the demonstrations was becoming more "popular," the Japanese who traditionally demonstrate—the membership of some militant unions and the militant Zengakuren groups from some universities—still gave the directions.

The assertion that the demonstrations were "national" in character is less easy to accept. Japan's rural population, conservative in politics as in most ways, is always suspicious of highjinks in the capital. The interpretations of the press emphasized urban unrest while giving little account to rural placidity.

there was a hint the police were serving to the Government's political advantage, the press reacted with an emotionalism so intense
that dispassionate reporting cracked beneath it.

Another obsession in the press was the *uyoku,* or Right-wing.
Kazuo Kuroda, a writer for the *Japan Times,* has said that

> most intellectuals, including newspaper editors and commen-
> tators, have a sort of guilt complex concerning *uyoku* ide-
> ologies. . . . If the *uyoku* means lack of reason rather than true
> patriotism, Leftist intellectuals are essentially not much differ-
> ent from the *uyoku* in being motivated by a hidden emotional
> complex.

As in the case of the police, the press has a tendency to distort
stories in which the *uyoku* is involved.[7] The term is so odious that
sayoku (Left-wing) is almost never used. "Progressive forces" is
used instead, except for the Trotskyite wing of Zengakuren when it
is particularly anarchistic.

Two examples of this hyper-sensitivity are the coverages given
the June 4 general strike by the *Asahi* and the June 15 "united
action" by the *Yomiuri.* The *Asahi,* even though Right-wing activists
had been of no significance up through June 4, said two reasons
the general strike was without violence were that "not one police-
man could be seen in many of the [railroad] stations" and that
"Right-wing unpleasantness was only sporadic." On June 15, the
situation had changed and Right-wingers did appear, driving a
truck into demonstrating Zengakuren students and then attacking
them with clubs. This happened at 2:50 p. m., according to the
Yomiuri, and at 5:20 p. m., according to the *Asahi.* A little after
5:00 p. m. Zengakuren students broke into the Diet compound and
began fighting the police. The *Yomiuri* subsequently stated flatly
in its news story that the day's chain of violence had been set off
by the Right-wingers. The *Asahi,* which had tempered its reporting
after June 4, said only that Right-wingers had clashed with demonstrators; and it was careful to point out that Zengakuren violence
had begun in the Diet compound *before* the attack from Right-
wingers.

---

[7] Japanese journalism often defends its "unbiased" anti-Government bias
by citing the coercion and censorship of the militarist area. The shrill frenzy
of the response to police and *uyoku* activities, however, would seem to indicate,
as Kuroda suggests, that many journalists today are trying to compensate for
what they left unsaid and undone in the 1930s and 1940s. On the other
hand, were they not vehement the penchant for Government authoritarianism
in Japan might be more apparent than it already is.

In addition to the police and *uyoku*, the United States seemed to be a sensitive subject to the *Asahi* on occasion. (Perhaps it would be better to say one part of the *Asahi* found it sensitive; the coverage was notably inconsistent.) Several times during the Treaty struggle, demonstrations held in front of the American Embassy were featured far out of importance to their news value, as if to emphasize, incorrectly and in contrast to the coverage by the *Mainichi* and *Yomiuri,* that popular indignation was directed as much against the United States as against Kishi and the Treaty.

On May 21, for example, evening editions carried the usual round-up story of demonstrations that had been held that day in various places throughout the city. As always most of the demonstrators went to the Diet (about 10,000) and a much smaller group to Kishi's residence. Some then went on to the American Embassy. The *Mainichi* gave the Embassy demonstration only two lines in its story, saying ". . . representatives from various provincial districts went to Kishi's residence with a petition, and when they were told he was not there, about 600 went to the American Embassy." The Embassy demonstration was considered insignificant by the *Yomiuri* and was not mentioned at all in its story. The *Asahi*, however, reversed the coverage and gave the Diet demonstration a small play beneath a large headline and picture on the Embassy demonstration. The writer did not have much to recount, since little had happened, but he was ecstatic with what he did have. The article began by saying, "Again people from all over the country came to Tokyo to take part." It then mentioned there were only 300, but that they came from districts as far away as Kansai and the Tohoku. Their vigor seemed to make up for their numbers:

> Every one of them was wearing a headband saying "crush the Security Treaty" and a chest banner saying "overthrow the Kishi Cabinet and dissolve the Diet." Every one of them was yelling, "I'm against the Security Treaty." They raised their spirits with the "Song of the People's Independence Movement."

That was about all there was to the story. In fact it is not surprising the writer had to fill up the space beneath the large headline and picture with slogans.

After the general strike, June 4, a large demonstration was held at the Diet, and again a few demonstrators went to Kishi's residence and the American Embassy. In its morning edition the next day the *Asahi* carried a large Page 1 story with a picture featuring the Embassy demonstration. The *Mainichi* carried a medium-sized demonstration story on Page 11 that featured the Diet and gave a small paragraph towards the end to the demonstration at the Embassy. The *Yomiuri* ran a small story on all the demonstrations on Page 11 that contained one line on the Embassy.

The Size of the Demonstrations

It is interesting to note, however, that the *Asahi* did not exaggerate the number of demonstrators at the Embassy, May 21 (300 as compared to the *Mainichi's* figure of 600), even though it overplayed the story.

In the evening editions of May 26, for example, the *Mainichi* and *Yomiuri* quoted the figures of the People's Council for the participants in the "united action" that day: 150,000 in Tokyo and two million throughout the country; while the *Asahi* used neither of the large figures and instead listed the participants according to their affiliations (for example, 6,000 from Zengakuren's Trotskyite wing, 7,000 from its Yoyogi wing), which was much less impressive. The following morning all three papers quoted the Council's new figure of 175,000 in Tokyo, but *only* the *Asahi* also included the police estimate of 60,000. In the same way in its morning edition, June 16, the *Mainichi* reported 20,000 students from Zengakuren's Trotskyite wing had led the assault into the Diet grounds the day before; the *Yomiuri* reported 10,000 and the *Asahi* 7,000.

The *Asahi* often did not use the Council's figures, and when it did, it almost always ran the police estimate (about half as large on the average) beside them. In contrast, the *Mainichi* always used the Council's inflated figures and the *Yomiuri* generally did. In other words, despite its other efforts to prove the demonstrations had a wide base of support, the *Asahi* was by far the most accurate in reporting the actual size of the demonstrations.

The period of strong support in the press for the demonstrations was at its height, June 4. The build-up in the three newspapers for the general strike was extensive. On June 1 the *Mainichi* said at

The June 4 General Strike

least four million people could be expected to take part, and on June 2 the *Yomiuri* predicted 3.5 million participants.

None of the three papers faced directly the issue of the strike's illegality.[8] The *Asahi* warned June 1, that participation by the public railroad workers would be illegal, but in examining the matter editorially June 3, it managed to condone the strike as planned by Sohyo. The editorial said: "We do not agree with a disorderly protest strike," but it claimed this was "not the direct action" usually associated with a general strike. Rather it said it would have

> the same character as the meetings and mass demonstrations which have been held repeatedly. In place of a demonstration there will be a walkout of a fixed duration in order to express a protest. . . . Before the Kishi Cabinet labels this protest strike by workers illegal, it should clearly state to the nation its [own] political responsibility.

The *Mainichi* disregarded the strike's illegality and made a direct appeal to the public for support. To those who would be affected by the train stoppage, its column the morning of June 4 said: "If you think this kind of 'real' power is justified, then you should support the protest. In order to achieve an important goal one may be temporarily inconvenienced."

All three papers called for restraint, fearing that if the strike became a "mob action" it would have the opposite effect from the one intended and, in the words of the *Mainichi,* only serve to allow Kishi once again to use this "best excuse" for not resigning. The *Mainichi* and *Yomiuri,* however, were less apologetic for the strike than the *Asahi* even though they condoned it in theory. The *Yomiuri* said editorially June 3: "If the action even remotely causes fears about parliamentarianism, it will certainly reverse public opinion against the progressive camp." It added in its column the morning of the strike that

> [In the *Asahi* poll, June 3] 58% of the people said they thought the Kishi Cabinet should be changed, but those who will support this use of "real" power by Sohyo will not be 58% of the country. Some of this 58% of the populace, these "voiceless voices," can support neither Kishi . . . nor the strike. Therefore the strike today will show which side has more support

---

[8] By law public workers cannot strike for political purposes. Sohyo had made its public railroad union, however, the heart of the strike. The Socialists argued with them that the proposed three-hour stoppage of trains would have a far greater effect on the public's attitude towards the Treaty than demonstrations could have.

among the people, the Government and the Government Party or Sohyo and the Opposition Party.

The *Asahi* column the same morning was more convinced what the results of the strike would be if violence could be avoided:

> How will the people receive this? The Kishi Cabinet is insolent, yet . . . if they [the strikers] have the understanding and cooperation of the people and the success is without violence, the increase in pressure against the Government will probably be opportune. If it ends in failure, the limits of so-called "extraparliamentary pressure" will be transparent. With this in mind we must be vigilant against disturbances of Left and Right-wing extremists.

The "largest railway strike since the war," another "united action" of the People's Council Against the Security Treaty, was given wider play in the press than any event since the May 19 forced vote. The *Mainichi*, using Sohyo's figures in its lead story, said "4,600,000 unionists and one million students, members of people's groups, and small businessmen" took part.

All papers praised the orderliness of the strike, which, they argued, showed the public had supported it. The *Mainichi's* column, June 5, called the strike a successful expression of public opinion, and its editorial, perhaps confusing Zengakuren's past performances with those of the public at large, said the strike showed "an increase in the good sense of the masses." It also said the lack of complaints from commuters was proof the public either "appreciated the objectives" of the strike or "held the same feelings" as the strikers. Because there had not been any violence, the column went on, Kishi "should immediately take advantage of this opportunity [to resign]." The illegality of the strike was again overlooked.

The *Yomiuri's* column, the night after this "largest railway strike," contented itself with a discourse on National Teeth Hygiene Week, which had also begun June 4, but its cartoon showed disgruntled commuters bringing their complaints to Kishi rather than to the railway strikers. Its editorial the next day admitted of the strike, while praising it, that "many problems remain concerning its legality." But its June 5 column pointed out these problems were not really of major concern:

> The June 4 political strike may have been illegal under the Public Workers Law, but it should be said that that law is directed against meetings protesting the politics of the nation.

> Yesterday's united action was something like a general strike,
> but it lies in the watershed of public opinion as both the Gov-
> ernment and Sohyo have said.

The *Asahi,* remembering Kishi's accusation that the press was not
representative of public opinion and that the "voiceless voices"
were behind him, pointed out in its editorial, June 5, that the only
way it could have been orderly was with the support of the general
public.

In short, the three national papers were so obsessed with the
downfall of the Kishi Cabinet they were willing to excuse a Sohyo
strike that was clearly illegal. They never quite supported it openly,
and in fact during the next few weeks the *Yomiuri* in particular
denounced Sohyo for the strike. But at the time, the exigencies of
the moment were obviously more persuasive than the law, because,
as the *Asahi* said, "the increase in pressure against the Government"
would "be opportune."

The reasoning of the apologists was based on their assertion that
the Diet no longer represented the national will. Thus the real
intention of the Public Workers Law—to forbid "meetings protest-
ing the politics of the nation"—was not necessarily being trespassed
upon by the railroad strike. This reasoning and the emotional urge
to accept exigencies that seemed opportune began to lose their
force in the press after June 4. The demonstrations grew worse and
when Hagerty's car was attacked at Haneda, June 10, all three
papers were aware there had been a definite planned shift in the
Left's campaign which they had supported in its earlier focus
against Kishi.

The June 15 Riot

The "united action" held June 11 was not given much comment
because interest still centered on the attack on Hagerty the day
before. The "united action" four days later, June 15, took place at
a time when Eisenhower's visit had become as crucial as the campaign against the Government. The previews in the press, which
was busy reporting Eisenhower's arrival in Manila, were compara-
tively minor. The *Mainichi's* editorial warned that morning that "it
should be borne in mind that the manifestation of true strength
depends on the lack of riotous behavior," but all three papers were

far less preoccupied with what would happen than they had been on May 26 and June 4.

During the chaos on June 15 Hosei University students were attacked by about 50 Right-wingers; Zengakuren members burned police trucks and broke into the Diet grounds; the police used tear gas for the first time and also for the first time were free with their night sticks when they drove the students back; and a Tokyo University woman student was trampled to death.

In all, 400 required hospitalization.

The national papers referred to the day as a "tragedy," and, in general, their coverage was complete, undramatic, and uncolored. Their treatment of the actions of the demonstrators, the police, and the Right-Wingers (with the exception of the *Yomiuri* on the latter) was equal and without bias. Obviously their approach had changed remarkably since May 20. Successively it had passed through violent indignation, apprehension, complacency, and support for an illegal strike, shock, and finally indignation again. But this time the indignation was not directed solely against the Government.

Violence

From April 13 to June 13, during demonstrations, 612 policemen were injured. The press' view of the violence that produced this varied as the struggle against the Government progressed. In the initial period, during the first week after the forced vote, condemnation centered on Zengakuren attacks on Kishi's residence. The *Asahi*, in a column, May 22, demanding that violence be done away with, pointed out that "the Opposition does not seem to have the power or inclination to do that." During the second phase, between the May 26 and June 4 strikes, there was fear violence would grow. A *Mainichi* editorial, May 29, said that

> besides an irregular Diet the thing we are most anxious about is that the movements against the Treaty are becoming too violent. . . . The movements against the Treaty must be conducted within the framework of law and democracy.

On May 31 the same paper said that its letters to the editor had showed a marked shift from concern with the forced vote to concern over the increasing violence countenanced by the Socialist Party.

Between June 4 and June 10, the press grew more outspoken in holding the Socialists responsible for violence. This was especially true of the attack on Hagerty, which had a strong effect on the three newspapers. This seemed to precipitate the change in sentiment which a week later produced the joint statement against violence published by 55 newspapers throughout the country. The *Mainichi,* in its column, June 11, called the attack on Hagerty "thoughtless violence" and an action of the pre-Meiji era. It said it was perfectly right to express opposition to the Treaty, but that "to turn those expressions into violence absolutely cannot be allowed." The *Asahi's* column the same morning said that after "such primitive behavior it is impossible [for Japan] to face the world." The *Yomiuri's* column, June 11, called the attack "extreme violence" and senseless as well, since Hagerty "did not come to study the state of affairs in Japan." Its column the next day claimed the people as a whole were responsible, because the politicians were their elected officials, and said violence to a foreign official was "unallowable" even though it had been the work of a small number of people. With detachment it noted that "because Japanese politics has 'too little tea in it', the behavior of the people is also 'without tea' [unreasonable]." [9]

After June 10 the editorial attacks on violence increased. Yet the assault on Hagerty had concerned the press almost more because it was "primitive" and would disgrace Japan internationally than because it was in itself an act of violence. The title of the *Asahi's* editorial, June 11, for example, had been "Behavior That Wounds National Pride." Like those of the *Mainichi* and *Yomiuri,* its main sentiment was one of embarrassment. By June 15, however, apologetics for the Left had all but disappeared. In their editorials, June 16, all three papers used *sayoku* (Left-wing) as an epithet for those who had fought against the police the day before.

The *Asahi* was still the least forceful in its criticism and the *Yomiuri* the most forceful. The *Asahi* said its expectations for an orderly demonstration "had been betrayed" and that Zengakuren's "breaking in through the South Gate [of the Diet] was not accidental; it could have been an action planned beforehand." It said the demonstrators were "a mob" and that the demonstration was "a bloody disaster,"

---

[9] This was the first time the "people" had been held responsible for anything. Significantly it was the *Yomiuri* that first discovered that "leaders" could not be blamed for everything.

more alarming than anything to date. . . . As for not believing in parliamentary democracy, the Right and the Left are the same. . . . If this should continue the Right and the Left-wings will more and more make use of force in their clashes. . . . It was that way in Germany just before the Nazis emerged.

The editorial noted rather bitterly that "Sohyo has lost control of the movement" and ended "strongly demanding self-reflection" on the part of Zengakuren.

The *Mainichi,* less embittered personally, attempted to find a middle ground from which everyone could be criticized. It said the Leftists were wrong in claiming the police had provoked the outbreak of violence, but admitted the Rightists might have had something to do with it. It added from a distance: "However, it is said that some Zengakuren leaders had planned to force a protest meeting within the Diet compound." It blamed the Government for their arrogant manner since the attack on Hagerty, and said "it is not impossible to interpret Zengakuren's actions as an impulsive reaction to this." On the other hand, it found all political leaders, those of the Government and Opposition alike, "soft-headed" in their understanding of social matters. It said most of the nation "looks on the clashes between Zengakuren and the police from a third position."

> One way of thinking says that because the Kishi Cabinet's politics are bad, even the use of force is permissible in opposing them. This is absolutely wrong. . . . We attack the undemocratic methods of the Kishi Cabinet. At the same time, the use of violence in opposition is absolutely unacceptable.

The editorial said the most important thing now was for "both sides to reflect dispassionately on their actions."

The *Yomiuri* editorial, being concerned neither with former delusions nor straddling, was not painful to read as the other two were. It said the People's Council and Sohyo were responsible for the riot and said that, "like the Hagerty incident, one group of extremists [Zengakuren] brought it on." Excessive use of force by the police and the actions of the Right-wingers were also significant, it said, but the "insane and barbarous" behavior of Zengakuren had been the direct cause. "The Socialist Party," it summed up, "has lost its independence and is being used by those who make violence their creed." The *Yomiuri's* column in the evening edition, June 16, was even more acute. Better than any other article during the Treaty struggle it described the dangers of the relativistic approach of the press (and much of the public) which confused motive with effect.

> At the time of the May 15 [1932] and February 26 [1936] incidents [10] it was said: "the action was wrong but the motives were purely patriotic." . . . Even among those who criticize Zengakuren's actions there are many who approve of its motives. In short, they reason that the methods of the Kishi Cabinet . . . brought this [the June 15 riot] on. It is completely meaningless. The argument that criticizes violence, and then says "however" and goes on to affirm the motive is exceptionally dangerous. Whatever its reasons, whatever its forms or methods, whatever brings it into being—violence must still be absolutely rejected. A country governed by law cannot allow a "however." Of course the *uyoku* and the attitudes of the police cannot be overlooked, but it is my opinion Zengakuren had planned from the beginning to use violence to force its way into the Diet compound.
>
> Japan today is controlled by a vicious circle; violence is used against violence. Coming in the wake of the Haneda incident, the incident last night was characterized by some foreign newspapers as "Japan on the eve of revolution," and when you look at it on the surface, it does appear near to that.
>
> Is the Japanese nation so slovenly it can be shaken by the fists of a few young military officers, or even students?

---

[10] Both were important dates in the ascendency of the militarists. The "5.15 incident" was a day of assassinations and other terrorist acts by young officers. The "2.26 incident" was an attempted coup in which several junior officers marched their battalion into Tokyo and seized control of strategic centers. The June 15, 1960, Zengakuren putsch at the Diet is now known as the "6.15 incident".

VII. EISENHOWER'S VISIT CANCELLED

In an editorial, May 12, the *Mainichi* pointed out two reasons President Eisenhower's pending visit was of great significance. First, Eisenhower's personality placed him "above" United States policies, making his visit the ideal one for a celebration of the centennial of Japan-United States relations; and second, it would be a honor to have him relax in Japan after his trip to the summit and the U.S.S.R. in the efforts of peace. Within a week both of these factors had changed. The summit had collapsed and Eisenhower's trip to the U.S.S.R. had been cancelled because (in the view of the Japanese press) of harsh cold war tactics on the part of the United States. At the same time, Eisenhower's visit to Japan could no longer be considered "above" United States policies.

Prime Minister Kishi himself had politicized the President's state visit by his timing of the forced vote in the Lower House. By superimposing the date of Eisenhower's arrival on the date when the forced vote would automatically become the opinion of the Diet, he had made it impossible for the visit to be detached from the struggle over the Treaty itself, that is, from internal politics.

Several parties took advantage of this fact. On the one side, Kishi attempted to overcome hostility to himself and his coup by making use of Eisenhower's international prestige; and on the other side, the extreme Left and the Japan Communist Party attempted to damage Eisenhower's international prestige, and America's position in Japan, by making use of the hostility towards Kishi. In the end both sides were partially successful: Kishi had the Treaty ratified, and the extreme Left created a greater show of anti-Americanism than they possibly could have hoped for before May 19.

Outside of Leftist dialecticians and some dissenting Liberal-Democrats, there was no mass sentiment against the Treaty in 1959. In the early spring of 1960, however, the Left (aided by the press' obsessional attacks on Kishi) was able to translate some of the existing anti-Kishi sentiment into a vague distrust of the Treaty. After Kishi's use of police and a forced vote in the Lower House; May 19, the Left's task was made much easier. But even then, when it had become apparent the Treaty would become law within a month, the increase in the size of the demonstrations and the support for them cannot be interpreted as a proportionate increase in anti-Treaty sentiment. As the *Asahi* said in an editorial, June 7: "Even the police say that since May 20, sentiment against Kishi has become far more widespread than the sentiment that existed against the Security Treaty."

Considering the importance of emotionalism and personality in Japanese politics, it is not surprising the dreary Diet deliberations early in 1960 aroused little popular interest for or against the Treaty. The Opposition, which did have an ideological disagreement with the Treaty, was only able to turn the vague distrust for the Treaty into popular passion after May 19; and the real object of the passion, when it was massive and more or less subscribed to by other than the organized Left, was Kishi and his methods. It is with this in mind that the timing of the vote—calculated by Kishi to be advantageous, yet potentially a gratuitous advantage to those interested in anti-Americanism—must be viewed.

As was pointed out earlier, the *Yomiuri* was the first of the three papers to explore these aspects of the May 19 Diet coup. Discussion of the issue did not become widespread until May 26, however, when the "united action" that day gave confidence to the Socialists and increased the press's support for their actions.

But from the beginning the press was wary of any tendency by the public to equate the United States with Kishi and his methods, a tendency which elements of the Left exploited less and less subtly as time went on. The *Mainichi's* column May 27 said:

> If America should side with the Kishi Cabinet there is fear that antipathy for Kishi will also become antipathy for the U. S. This unfortunate possibility must be escaped at all costs. Today it is a fact that the desire for Kishi to resign has become

linked with feelings against the Security Treaty.[1] However, we want America not to be confused by this and to view it dispassionately and with sophistication. We think those in Japan who desire an end to Kishi's power confuse that feeling with our friendship with America.

Later both the *Yomiuri* and *Asahi* condemned the tendency with particular reference to the role of the Socialists. The *Yomiuri*, as usual, was less tender with the Socialists; the *Asahi* criticized them but implied they were only slight in error. The *Yomiuri's* column the evening of June 7 said that

> Although the Socialist position is not specifically anti-American, its nuances are close to it. . . . It does not have to be said that Ike was invited by Japan. Even though the Socialists may be against the visit, the line cannot be taken that these opinions can be expressed directly to the President and Mr. Hagerty.
> At this time it would be sensible to postpone the visit. Even voices in the Government Party and in various Government quarters are calling for it. . . . But to take the national sentiment against Kishi and the doubts that exist about the Security Treaty and, as is, naively tie them to anti-Americanism would be soft-headed. . . . Both [the Government and Socialists] are acting as juveniles.

An *Asahi* editorial June 8 said of the Socialists:

> It is only strange they do not fear the fearfulness of what they give birth to. . . . We cannot have the Socialist Party transforming anti-Kishi sentiment into anti-American sentiment. No matter how much disagreement there is with the Security Treaty, Japan will not become anti-American.
> If this difference is not clearly pointed out, Japan will probably be held in contempt by much of the world. The figure of our parliamentarianism seems to be faltering. If the Socialist Party does not also watch its step, it will be dangerous.

The three papers all demanded something be done to de-politicize Eisenhower's visit so that Kishi and the Socialists could not continue to exploit it to their own ends. They suggested a ten-day recess of

---

[1] This is a revealing admission, for the press, at least through silence if nothing else, had been a leader in confusing "the desire for Kishi to resign" with "feelings against the Security Treaty." The Socialists' campaign (theoretical as usual) was directed against the Treaty, the press's against Kishi; but the press equivocated on direct action, for example, because they thought it was one of the few ways to force the Kishi Cabinet to resign. In other words they abetted the Socialists' campaign against the Treaty by not clearly divorcing their emotional *idée fixe* from the Treaty itself.

the Diet to separate the dates of Eisenhower's arrival and the Treaty ratification. The *Yomiuri* in a column, June 2, suggesting that Kishi felt he needed the Treaty ratified by the time Eisenhower came, said that, "the only thing hindering a recess is the personal obligation Kishi feels towards Eisenhower's impending visit." Then when a recess seemed unlikely, the press proposed the visit be postponed. The *Mainichi* in particular felt reluctant to do this. In an editorial, June 5, it said: "Certainly when one considers the automatic passage of the Treaty on the day of Ike's arrival, one realizes the situation grows worse every day"; and in an editorial the following day it reemphasized that postponement was "difficult" and could "not be considered lightly." But, it went on,

> not only do we feel that this [automatic ratification on the day of Eisenhower's arrival] complicates the situation for the worse, but it gives the impression the President's visit has a special political purpose. This may cause trouble for the President.

The editorial concluded that the state visit "decidedly is not now opportune" and that Kishi's stand on principle in regard to the trip was "dangerous" both to internal politics and future relations with America.

> The attitude . . . Prime Minister Kishi has displayed with excessive dogmatism is his intention to color the voices raised against the Government in a deliberately one-sided way. . . . [He] states positively that those who argue against the new Security Treaty are people who pray for a rupture in U. S.-Japan relations. . . . [He] sows the seeds that are causing anti-American sentiment. We have warned countless times that the anti-Kishi agitation spreading not only in the Opposition Parties but in the country at large must not become anti-Americanism.
>
> In Prime Minister Kishi's extreme words the nature of the movements critical of the Kishi Government is given a deliberately distorted interpretation. It makes one fear it is done the better to precipitate this dangerous situation.

The *Yomiuri's* editorial the same day examined the Socialists' manipulation of Eisenhower's visit as well as Kishi's. It "demanded vigilance" against the anti-American efforts of Sohyo and the Socialists and said that Socialist Secretary-General Asanuma's claim the visit was "interference in internal politics" went "to extremes."

> Ike was invited to visit Japan by the Japanese Government. Whether Prime Minister Kishi's methods are good or bad is

something else again, but since Ike's visit comes at the invitation of our Government, why is it called interference?

Let's look at it the other way. If, for example, Ike conceded to the requests of the Socialist Party and cancelled his trip, it would plainly be a blow to the Kishi Cabinet. Thus in that case the Socialist Party would be using the power of a foreign country to wound the Government of its own country. . . . Secretary-General Asanuma's declaration is mistaken. . . . It is said that he who chases a deer does not see the mountain.

The *Yomiuri* went on to say it thought the trip should be cancelled because it did not feel a foreign head of state could be properly received in the present atmosphere.

It may be, as those opposing the Government say, that the Government has gone so far as to use Ike's visit as a lever to aid the Kishi Government. If that is so, the outrage is being committed by the Kishi Cabinet, for Ike is not that kind of person.

The national papers were concerned that United States-Japan relations would suffer from the partisan maneuverings over the visit, and during the period before Hagerty's arrival, articles and interpretations discussing the subject increased. In political cartoons, Eisenhower's visit even replaced Kishi as a topic of interest. (Between May 27 and June 10, eight of the twenty-nine political cartoons were on Eisenhower, five on Kishi, and three on Eisenhower and Kishi together. The *Asahi* published seven of the eleven that featured Eisenhower or Eisenhower and Kishi together.)

One part of the discussion centered on the real meaning of the visit from the United States point of view, which, the press felt, could clarify the extent to which the visit was being adapted by Kishi and the Socialists. Accordingly, the *Asahi* on June 7 featured a large Page 1 cable from its New York correspondent that quoted *Newsweek* as saying Eisenhower was making the trip so the Kishi Cabinet would not fall, in other words to bolster the Kishi Cabinet. Considering the hostility towards Kishi this was certain to bring a reaction, which it did. Long before Kishi had politicized Eisenhower's visit the *Yomiuri* had said Kishi's aim was, "to perpetuate his regime on the basis of the new Security Treaty"; now it appeared to the press that the United States was going to help Kishi perpetuate his unpopular regime through Eisenhower's visit.

The *Asahi* criticized United States policy on two points: because it supported Kishi simply to get the Treaty ratified, and because it misread the sentiment against Kishi in Japan. Its June 7 editorial said:

> The American Government gives the impression they would like to see the Kishi Government continue in power, and at the same time their observation is that the movement against the Kishi Cabinet is the work of a few people in Left-wing factions. . . . We think the movement against the Kishi Cabinet must not be enlarged so that it becomes an anti-American movement. This above all must be absolutely avoided. . . . [but] we firmly believe the introduction of police into the Diet and the unilateral vote, as well as Kishi's refusal to take responsibility for the political confusion that followed, is at the bottom of the parliamentary crisis. . . .
>
> America must never misinterpret this fact: saving parliamentary politics is without question the real problem behind demands for Kishi's ouster. . . . Even if Kishi withdraws, the Japanese people will remain, and for America the long-range source of friendly relations is the people. We would like Washington to consider this fact in earnest.

The *Mainichi* also was adamant over any interpretation that said the antipathy towards the Kishi Cabinet was minor. Its column, June 8, took American journalism to task:

> American newspapers are taking the position that the present unrest is caused by a small number of Left-wingers and Communists. If Ike's visit is called off, they are afraid it will appear he gave in to these pressures.
>
> This viewpoint is very dangerous. The *New York Times* has said that, "the best way to save the Prime Minister should be considered." If this becomes [the American viewpoint], there is danger that sentiment hostile to Kishi will be indiscriminately redirected against America.

The *Yomiuri* said in its column June 6 that because Eisenhower's trip had been "tied to politics . . . the danger of anti-Kishi sentiment becoming anti-American has grown." Like the *Asahi* it empahsized that, "beyond the political and diplomatic level, the relationship between Japan and the United States is extremely close," and said that an Eisenhower trip to support Kishi would not aid friendly relations. Because of the circumstances, the column added cynically, "it would probably serve friendly relations more if, rather than inviting Ike, the Boston Symphony were invited again."

The Attack on Hagerty

It is apparent the "big three" national papers strongly opposed the Socialist tendency to foster anti-American sentiment out of the anti-Kishi campaign. Slogans against President Eisenhower's visit had first appeared in the May 26 "united action," and after that the three-part demand of every Sohyo-Socialist demonstration was: "down with Kishi, dissolve the Diet, and cancel Eisenhower's visit." The *Mainichi* and *Yomiuri* were apt to find equal fault with what they considered both Kishi's and the Socialists' distortions of the visit (as well as what they regarded as the United States's inaccurate view); the *Asahi* found fault with both, but to them it seemed Kishi's distortions were those "done the better to precipitate this dangerous situation."

The turning point in the anti-American insinuations came June 10, when Eisenhower's press secretary, James Hagerty, arrived at Tokyo's Haneda Airport to make final arrangements for the President's visit. Hagerty was met at the airport by Ambassador MacArthur, but their car was immediately surrounded and assaulted by Zengakuren students and unionists. The police were unable to free the car and eventually a Marine helicopter had to pick up the party and fly them to the Embassy. That night Asanuma gave the official Socialist interpretation: "Mr. Hagerty drove his car at full speed into the midst of the students and unionists, and a helicopter was ready for him." The main interest of the attack, however, is not the Socialists' inability to recognize or acknowledge what had really happened, but rather the composition of the group that barricaded Hagerty.

The demonstration at the airport included approximately 1,500 Zengakuren students and 5,000 unionists; leading the assault were the students and several hundred employees of the Japan Steel Tube Company's Kawasaki plant (Kanagawa Prefecture), which is not far from the airport. This Kawasaki local is one of the most radical locals in the *Tekko Roren* union, which is a member of Sohyo. The local's leadership is nominally not Communist, but it is extreme and quite possibly open to Communist direction on occasion.

As for the students in the assault, they were *all* members of the anti-leadership or Yoyogi wing of Zengakuren,[2] which is closely affiliated with the Japan Communist Party. The leadership or Trotskyite wing of Zengakuren did not bother to send students to Haneda June 10—when Hagerty was the target—yet it had been the Trotskyite and not the Yoyogi wing that rioted at Haneda January 16, 1960, the day Kishi left to sign the Treaty in Washington. In fact, throughout the struggle against the Treaty the Trotskyite wing took *no* particular interest in the anti-Eisenhower campaign.

The Hagerty attack, on the other hand, was the Yoyogi wing's *initial* use of violence during the Treaty struggle; prior to that they had held only quiet demonstrations. Their violent behavior that day, therefore, takes on special significance as an obvious Communist Party tactic. Following the June 10 incident, the new pattern of the Yoyogi wing was set and its use of violence increased, but the violence had a particular object: anti-Americanism. After the "united action" at the Diet June 11, for example, the Trotskyite wing went on to demonstrate at Kishi's residence, its favorite non-Diet site. The Yoyogi wing went straight to the American Embassy.

The national papers reacted differently to the Yoyogi wing's attack on Hagerty and its implications. The *Yomiuri* and *Mainichi* emphasized the special character of the violence, while the *Asahi* did not. This was true both in news coverage and editorial comment. In the evening editions of June 10, for example, both the *Asahi* and *Yomiuri* ran main headlines of "Hagerty Stalled at Diet"; under this headline the *Asahi* said, "Right-wingers, Workers, Police Clash," while the *Yomiuri* said, "Encircled by Zengakuren Members of Anti-Leadership Wing." Both the *Yomiuri* and *Mainichi* carried pictures of the assault on Hagerty's car; the *Asahi* carried only a portrait of Hagerty. The *Mainichi* and *Yomiuri* also emphasized in their lead stories the fact that the student attackers were members of Zenga-

---

[2] Zengakuren is divided into two groups that have little to do with each other. The larger of the two is called the leadership or Trotskyite wing; it attacks the police and Communist Party headquarters with equal abandon. It has no connections with the Communist Party, which it calls revisionist, nor with international Communism, which it considers as bourgeois and imperialistic as the free world. The violent demonstrations conducted by "Zengakuren" prior to June 10 were actually made up only of students from the Trotskyite wing. Their object throughout was Kishi himself, and when the wing was not attacking the Diet they were assaulting Kishi's private residence. The Trotskyite wing led the breakthrough into the Diet compound June 15, and the woman student who was killed was a member of its wing. The anti-leadership or Yoyogi wing is so-called because its members are always being thrown out of Zengakuren-wide council meetings and because Communist Party headquarters in Tokyo is in Yoyogi. It refers to the leadership wing as Blanquist.

kuren's Yoyogi (Communist Party) Wing; the *Asahi* did not mention this fact at all and in general underplayed the violence at Haneda.

The following morning the *Asahi* apparently realized it had ignored the violence too much and its lead story was devoted to it. The *Mainichi* and *Yomiuri*, having covered that aspect adequately the evening before, led with stories that Eisenhower's plans had not changed. In other stories the *Mainichi* and *Yomiuri* again emphasized that the attacking students were members of the anti-leadership Zengakuren wing; the *Asahi* mentioned the fact once towards the very end of its long lead story. All three papers carried a police estimate of the situation, but again the *Asahi*'s version differed. Both the *Mainichi*'s and *Yomiuri*'s stories repeated the police warning that the Yoyogi wing's action was the "first statement by the Communist Party" of a new danger. The *Asahi* ran the story on Page 1, but the assertions against the Communist Party were *not* included and there was no discussion of the significance of the anti-leadership Zengakuren wing's action. Instead the article throughout referred to the attackers only as "students."

The *Asahi* and *Mainichi* discussed the general aspects of the "embarrassing" Haneda incident in their editorials June 11, the *Mainichi* with somewhat more intensity. The *Yomiuri*, however, wrote directly on the significance of the attack. It noted that all of a sudden the Yoyogi wing had radically shifted its policies and suggested that the attack was part of a planned anti-American campaign. It said that the claim of "violence to protect democracy" was "absolutely impossible" to accept, since "those who run with criminals are criminals." It went on:

> One can think of many possible reasons for this change [in the tactics of the Yoyogi wing of Zengakuren]. But if it is recalled that the leadership wing has been opposed to using the anti-Treaty campaign as a [general] slogan, while the anti-leadership wing was designing a flag for anti-Americanism, then one understands why the anti-leadership group came forward with such force at this time.

The *Asahi* acted only after the other two papers had brought the facts to light. The following morning, June 12, it ran an article entitled, "Anti-American Struggle: Accidental or Planned?" Opinions on both sides were given, but without resolving them. There was no mention of the fact that the Yoyogi wing of Zengakuren was related to the Communist Party; in fact, there was no mention of the Communist Party whatsoever. The closest the article came to judging the question was by saying that the Yoyo-gi wing members "have probably gone astray from their position" of not tolerating violence. The *Mainichi* discussed the issue in a long and detailed article, June 14, which was less coy than the *Asahi's* but also less accusatory than the *Yomiuri* had been.

In short, while both the *Yomiuri* and *Mainichi* gave an answer to the question—accidental or planned?—the *Asahi* did not actually even examine the forces that might have planned it. Perhaps the *Asahi's* reaction had been like that of the "intellectuals," which the *Mainichi* described in a column, June 11, as: "It is hard to understand why students and members of the People's Council have resorted to such action!"

Cancellation

Following the Haneda incident, the *Yomiuri* and the *Asahi* re-iterated their beliefs that the trip should be cancelled in order for Eisenhower not to be "dragged into our political warfare." The *Yomiuri* said in a column, June 11, that "if there had not been the May 20 incident, a warm, truly national welcome for Ike would have materialized naturally and spectacularly." The *Asahi* in an editorial, June 14, made another plea for reconsideration:

> In regard to President Eisenhower's approaching visit, we want to request from the bottom of our hearts that the President look clearly, without a clouded eye, at the real factors operating in Japan.

The *Mainichi's* position was somewhat different. It feared the effects of the trip being cancelled more than it feared a possible worsening in United States-Japan relations if Eisenhower came. Its column, June 12, said, "We must welcome Eisenhower no matter what. If his visit were called off now, not only could it be called bowing to violence, but Japan's stature internationally would be lost." In an editorial the following day it said the reason Eisenhower's visit had become a partisan issue was "chiefly Prime Minister Kishi's clumsy parliamentary conduct," and it said "while most of the nation remains ignorant of it," the partisan use of Eisenhower's trip by both sides was "building conditions favorable to Japanese Communism." It called the Haneda incident an instance of "spreading Communism through osmosis," but found the demonstrations still predominantly anti-Kishi and anti-Treaty and not pro-Communist nor anti-American: "Rather, those who oppose Japanese Communism are probably in the majority."

On the morning of June 14 all three papers again editorially called for a Diet recess of a week to divorce the day of Eisenhower's arrival and the automatic ratification of the Treaty. The *Mainichi*, the only one of the three still advocating the visit, pointed out in a column that morning the reservations that remained. Eisenhower should be welcomed, it said.

> However, Prime Minister Kishi's responsibility should not be forgotten in the atmosphere of welcome. While a political truce is desirable, it should not be used to make a *fait accompli* out of the forced vote taken by the Liberal-Democratic Party on the Security Treaty. . . . Recognition of the Security Treaty must never be made a present for Ike. It is necessary that Prime Minister Kishi prove concretely that Ike's visit to Japan is divorced from the present political situation. If Kishi shows in the slightest way that he is using the visit to his advantage, the warm welcome will evaporate.

The following day Eisenhower's arrival in Manila was covered. The *Yomiuri* and *Mainichi* devoted about half their front pages to articles and pictures of the event, in addition to space on inside pages. Their coverage was approximately twice as extensive as the *Asahi*'s. The *Yomiuri* carried five pictures on the story, the *Mainichi* three, and the *Asahi* one. (Normally picture coverage is equal among the papers or slightly more extensive in the *Asahi*.)

That day, June 15, the Diet riot filled the evening editions and the editions the following day. The day after that, June 17, Kishi announced the "postponement"—which was tantamount to cancellation—of the President's visit and the three national papers (with the initiative of the *Asahi*'s Skintaro Ryu) published their joint declaration against violence. The four other major Tokyo papers joined them in the declaration—the *Sankei, Nihon Keizai, Tokyo Shimbun,* and *Tokyo Times*—as well as forty-eight newspapers outside the capital. The only major newspaper in the country not to join in the declaration was the Leftist-inclined *Hokkaido Shimbun.*

In their editorials and columns the morning of June 18 the national papers gave their reactions to the cancellation. Both the *Mainichi* and *Yomiuri*, emphasizing that the police had been unable to assure Eisenhower's safety, expressed relief because of the personal danger there might have been to Eisenhower from an individual act of terrorism. The *Asahi* did not discuss this aspect of the visit. The *Asahi* also differed from the other two on who had suffered from the cancellation of the visit. To the *Yomiuri* and the *Mainichi* it was "the trust and prestige of Japan in the free world"; to the *Asahi* it was Kishi. The *Yomiuri* and *Mainichi* severely criticized the Socialists as well as the Government for what had come to pass; the *Asahi* criticized only Kishi. The *Mainichi's* column said:

> The most wretched losers in this conflict are not Prime Minister Kishi and his clique. We must remember that. The trust and prestige of Japan in the free world have fallen. The leaders of the Communist countries are probably gloating over what has happened. . . .
>
> I ask a question of the Socialist Party. You say those members of Zengakuren who believe in destroying law and order are pitiful victims of the Kishi Government. Do you agree, then, with those who destroy law and order through group violence? But you also claim you are protecting democracy. There is no way both can be true. Which one do you really support?

The *Yomiuri's* column said there was no question the visit was not now opportune, but it went on to say that despite the embroilment of the visit in internal politics, "I believe we wanted to welcome America's President warmly from our hearts, and I believe even now we do." Like the *Mainichi*, it said it would take a long time for Japan to recover the international respect it had lost in the last month.

The *Yomiuri's* editorial pointed out, as did the *Mainichi*, that the sequence of events in Japan had abetted causes of the Communist bloc. As the paper had done increasingly in the last few weeks, it examined the Socialists without sentimentality:

> Of course it cannot be said that Kishi's political power is entirely responsible for bringing on what has happened. At the least, the thing that provided the direct opportunity for social unrest was the extreme Left's tendency to resort to violence, which they called "force." This is clear to everyone.

The *Asahi's* position contrasted sharply with those of the other two papers. Its editorial did not discuss the cancellation or attempt a survey of the last month, nor did it deal with the international significance of what had happened. Instead it presented a jejune plan for the two days remaining before the Treaty became law. The plan had three points, none of which was likely to come to pass and none of which did. They were: 1) a suspension of the Diet session, 2) "rapid normalization" of Diet affairs by the Government and Liberal-Democratic Party, and 3) a return to the Diet by the Opposition Parties which then were to "adjust their attitudes" to make way for cooperation. It requested "resolution and action" from "the Kishi Government's severe self-reflection," and at the same time demanded the pleasure of a public confession of sin by its *bête noire*: "Prime Minister Kishi should show in front of the nation that he feels his political responsibility."

The *Asahi*'s column did take up the cancellation of the visit, but it saw only its expedient effects. Its reading of the cancellation was also noticeably different from those of the *Mainichi* and *Yomiuri*:

> The cancellation of Ike's visit does not especially bother the nation. . . . The only thing that bothers the nation is that Prime Minister Kishi has made us lose faith all over the world. The decision came too late, but for long-range good relations between Japan and America, it was for the best. Anyway, it will probably kill the Kishi Cabinet.

Results of the Cancellation

The June 17 commentary of the *Mainichi* and *Yomiuri* was distinctly different from what it had been at any time since May 20. Considering the narrowness of purpose with which the press had waged its campaign against Kishi, it was almost surprisingly untendentious. Perhaps the combination of the June 15 rioting and the cancellation of Eisenhower's visit by terror had made a more incisive view possible. For the first time since the demonstrations began after the vote, for example, both papers pointed out that the sequence of events had been of service to the Communist bloc. It almost seems as if it had taken a day of anarchy and an international incident to overcome the obsessional preoccupation of the two papers with Kishi's downfall. Compared to the invective of the columns and editorials during the preceding month, the commentary, June 17, was so dispassionate it was somber.

The *Asahi*'s case can be explained less easily. Just as the *Yomiuri* was the most concerned of the three with uncovering machinations of the present disguised as "popular," the *Asahi* was the most concerned with uncovering machinations of the past directed against what was "popular." Even after the "6.15 incident" the *Asahi* was still, in general, apologistic for anti-Kishi excesses and attempted to rationalize the means to its end. In addition it disregarded the international significance of the cancellation of Eisenhower's visit, making no mention of its meaning to the cold war. Unlike the *Mainichi* and *Yomiuri*, which found Japan's trust and prestige in the free world the "wretched losers," the *Asahi* said only that "it will probably kill the Kishi Cabinet." In short, its opinions remained expedient.

VIII. CONCLUSIONS

The national papers began in 1960 with an anti-Kishi movement that later assumed much the same character as the anti-Treaty campaign of the organized Left. The three papers were not specifically against the Treaty; they were, however, against Kishi and his Government, and more particularly, against the way in which the Treaty was ratified.

The organized Left's opposition to the Treaty gathered widespread support only after the use of police in the Diet and the forced vote of May 19. Before that date the struggle against the Treaty was largely detached from the public and was the work of a concerted minority. But after May 19, a substantial number of the politically conscious were antagonistic to the forced vote, and, by extension, to the Kishi Government. The national papers were instrumental in intensifying this antagonism. Still the Treaty itself remained of secondary importance. Through the combined actions of Kishi and the Opposition, anti-Treaty sentiment increased in the country and particularly in Tokyo, by implication. The national papers were also instrumental in intensifying this implication.

By June 10—the day of the attack on Hagerty at Haneda—a further implication became evident: the attempt by the organized Left to push anti-Kishi sentiment beyond the anti-Treaty campaign into anti-Americanism (perhaps at bottom largely anti-Westernism). The mass dailies refused to accept this. They had condoned direct action through expediency, but they did not condone anti-Ameri-

[81]

canism even though it could have helped overthrow the Kishi Cabinet. In this the national papers showed they strongly resist the xenophobia renascent in some parts of Japanese society.

The Communist press throughout the world, and particularly that in mainland China, had conducted a concerted campaign against Kishi long before the revision of the Treaty had become a major political issue in Japan. Kishi had been portrayed as the embodiment of all past Japanese evils, the lackey of "American imperialism," and the leader of a return to "fascist militarism." As pointed out earlier, Socialist leaders had uncritically given their seals of approval to numerous joint declarations in Peking which laid a basis for linking together sentiment against Kishi, against the Treaty, and against the United States. The front organizations as well as the Communist Party in Japan played heavily on the peace issue in the combined opposition. When the "big three" of Japanese journalism were ready to link their fixation against Kishi with the opposition to the handling of the Treaty, many of the slogans and arguments were available, and here the Leftist influence in the management and unions of the newspapers obviously played an important role.

It is worth noting that so intense was the sentiment against Kishi and his failure to "adjust" that with rare exceptions the Japanese press failed to inform its readers that the revised Treaty was a decided step forward from the point of view of Japanese national interest. Here too the "big three" failed to evidence responsible and factual reporting on a key issue.

Within the Japanese public the anti-Kishi sentiment was of a dual nature: it was against the man and against the existing order. The first aspect was volatile, but the second is perhaps of more significance for the future. Discontent with the existing society is evident everywhere in Japan today. A popular movement against the existing order can therefore readily find a number of active supporters, especially among the young, and a larger number of passive sympathizers. In 1960, prior to the riot of June 15, the national papers helped lead such an attack. Because of their peculiar historical traditions (disregarding for a moment the cases of biased reporting), their editorial campaigns failed to take into account the plurality of positions that a free political system must accommodate. They worked themselves into an implicit "either-or" argument: either Kishi resigned or there would be violence. At the same time, they fomented the very division they lamented when it moved beyond control. They tried to represent public opinion as having a unanimity which it did not. Their own postwar inconsistencies are readily apparent, yet in the political sphere, ironically enough, they still adhere to a traditional desire for totality, that is, conformity.

It is doubtful whether subsequent events have affected very much the conviction held by the national dailies that they embody and articulate the public opinion of the whole Japanese nation. The election of November 20, 1960, which was contested primarily on the Treaty issue and on the events of the preceding spring, saw the return of the Liberal-Democrats with an even larger majority than Kishi had held. The results did not bear out claims by the national press that Japanese public opinion repudiated the policies of the party of Kishi. The November election results indicated the extent to which judgments about Japan based on events in the streets of Tokyo must be modified in generalizations about all of Japan. The "big three" failed to make such modifications, and the result in the case of the Treaty struggle was distortion and inaccuracy.

The three papers weighted their coverage of the Diet vote—the immediate cause of the turmoil that followed. They were together about equal in their campaigns against Kishi and the Government. In varying degrees they supported the extra-parliamentary activities of the Opposition, the *Asahi* maintaining its rationalizations longer than the other two.

All three were adverse to the effort to give the struggle an anti-American drift. The *Yomiuri* was the most outspoken against anti-Americanism; the *Mainichi* was aware of the drift but less lucid in describing it. The *Asahi* chose to hold uppermost the fact that Kishi had originally politicized Eisenhower's visit, and it therefore viewed Kishi as the primary object to the end. It gave less play to the probable Communist source of the attack on Hagerty, and, while opposing xenophobic anti-Americanism, largely ignored the tactical advantages of the drift to the Communist world. In general all three papers viewed the Treaty struggle from a narrow, national point of view. The meaning of the demonstrations to the world, and especially the significance of the cancellation of Eisenhower's visit, were largely overlooked until after the visit had been cancelled. And then it was the *Yomiuri* and the *Mainichi*, and not the *Asahi*, that emphasized what had happened.

The *Yomiuri* had colored Asanuma's role in the November 27, 1959, demonstration more than the other two papers, but throughout the crucial weeks of the struggle it was the least tendentious in its reporting. The *Mainichi* attempted to assume a middle-of-the-road position (among those opposing the Government), yet it consistently exaggerated the sizes of the demonstrations. The *Asahi* reported their numbers accurately while often overplaying those held at the American Embassy.

These and other such items show the inconsistencies among the mass dailies. But in general there were certain characteristics peculiar to each paper: in the *Yomiuri*, coloration—dramatized reporting but realistic commentary; in the *Mainichi*, "neutrality"—a Peiping propaganda release and a *New York Times* dispatch given equal consideration; and in the *Asahi*, an interplay of superior journalism and "progressive" advocacy—straight reporting (stories dealing with the police, and often the American Embassy, excepted) and apologetics for any movement against the existing order. Obviously biased reporting was represented in all three newspapers, perhaps through design, but it should be remarked that it was also erratic. This would make biased reporting appear to be the result of agreement among certain men who controlled specific editions. Certainly it was not a general practice even though it occurred more regularly with specific subjects.

The "non-partisan" principle of the Japanese press is admirable, but since such powerful newspapers can never be politically detached, it is also unrealistic. In practice the "independent" position of the three national dailies leads to advocacies that are almost purely *ad hoc*, and such sudden, headlong causes are in turn unusually susceptible to emotion and to prejudices inherited from the past. The emotion generally takes the form of a hunger for affixing responsibility for society's malaise; the prejudice most often evident is the "unbiased" anti-Government bias. Together this emotion and this prejudice can lead the press to subvert the democratic cause it professes, as it did during the Treaty struggle. The emotion is unseemly in responsible journalism, the prejudices out of place in postwar Japan. In technical and intellectual competence Japan's national papers rank high among the world's free presses, but their service in a democracy is endangered by these two weaknesses.

In short, the emotional reaction of the press to police intervention, considering Japan's recent history, is understandable, but this does not excuse the colored reporting of the May 19 Diet vote. In the same way fear of Government-Rightist collusion cannot excuse distorted coverage of Right-wing activities or failure to note the collusion of Left-wing activities with a campaign abetted by a foreign power. Editorially a newspaper is free to conduct any legal campaign and adopt any responsible position it wishes. The campaign against the Kishi Government was, of course, in itself legal, but condoning an illegal strike because it is opportune is at the very least irresponsible. The Japanese press, like Japanese society, is among the most free in the world. It is more free not only because it is unhampered by coercion or repressive laws, but because it is undeterred by the sense of restraint that comes with experience in freedom. A study of the role of the Japanese press in the Treaty struggle indicates only too clearly that it understands its freedom but not its responsibility.

In sum, there were many causes for the disorders in Japan in the spring of 1960. Outside forces had their part. But the important point is that there would have been dissatisfaction over events even if Kishi and the Left had not made anti-Westernism an issue.

Kishi himself was overbearing in the way he handled the Treaty ratification. His use of police in the Diet and his forced vote despite the initial violence on the part of the Opposition were strong-arm methods. In view of the international situation—the U-2 incident and the fiasco of the Paris summit meeting—they were more than inept. They indicated arrogance and a disregard for the sensibilities of his country and its cultural traditions of "adjustment." This cannot continue in postwar Japan. Despite the plurality the conservative party receives from the rural populace, a Japanese Government can no longer act without being sensitive to the sentiments of the people, including the minority parties and factions. The Japanese rural populace may always be conservative—it is likely that it will—but its vote will not always be automatic as it is now. Japan may have a conservative government for yet another decade, but in any case the *way* the Government is elected will change. It will not be elected through habit, but because it is responsive to the people. And when that comes about, there will be no place for arrogance on the part of the Government, even if it has an overwhelming majority.

The Socialists, dogmatic and prewar in their official thinking, will similarly not receive support for the same reasons they do now. By applying Marx's critique of 19th century England to 20th century Japan they are hopelessly irrelevant. The law of the increasing impoverishment of the masses is not even remotely true. The militant dialectics of the Socialist Party apply to fewer people, not more, as time goes on, for classes in Japan become less distinct as the country's energy spreads its prosperity into the hands of the many. Among intellectuals and the *Bunka* Establishment (journalists included) Leftist thought will probably continue to be *de rigueur* for some time, and the more inapplicable ("pure") it is, the more fashionable. But politicians and labor leaders will have to worry about votes, which are seldom attracted by theoretical niceties.

Legitimate unrest among the young—especially when they are students, before they go to work—sharpens the tone of the Left in Japan, but if the country's phenomenal economic success continues, the power of arguments based on doctrinaire anachronisms will probably prove as ineffective as it has become in Britain.

This is not to say that the majority of the younger generation —those under 35—do not want a radical change. In fact they do. But the change will be Japanese, one that will make use of Europe's 19th and early 20th centuries, and of Japan's 19th and early 20th centuries, but without the present Socialist over-emphasis on the former or the present conservative over-emphasis on the latter. If it is to work it will have to be at the same time autochthonic and new. Before the future comes there is of course the danger that the past will seize the present. There were intimations of it during the Treaty struggle. For the Government, the Opposition, and the press all suffered from one common malady. Each, in its own way, undermined democracy for the same reason: in deference to the past.

The hold of the past was obvious. In the psychodrama of just two months—May and June, 1960—it was apparent in both the rough display of power by the Government and in the violence of those outside the Government. However, youth—what counts in Japan—served its own ends. Being divorced from the past it is part lethargic, part reckless, but for different reasons than the rural farmer or the confirmed Leftist. More than anything else those who have come of age since the war wish for a *modus operandi* consonant with the present. Somewhat like Japan's youth, the national newspapers encounter unauthoritarian society with excess and experimentation.

The task of Japanese youth is to build a moral basis for society, to replace that which crumbled in the hands of their parents. The influence of 37 million newspapers in times of crisis, particularly of the three national papers, will remain vital. If the national papers surmount their penchant for emotion and their outdated prejudice, their influence will be efficacious when next the existing order is tested. On the other hand, should they refuse to lead through example as well as through slogans, the outcome could be even more serious than in 1960 when the Socialist Secretary-General was assassinated and there were attempted assassinations of another Socialist leader and of Kishi himself. For the murder of Asanuma in October, 1960, and the attempts on the lives of Jotaro Kawakami in June and Kishi in July, 1960, all came from the same cause—the revival of direct action as a legitimate means for changing the social order. Assassination and violence, the twin deliverers of direct action, are ancient evils in Japan. Twenty-five years ago Japan changed cabinets by assassination. Moderation and deliberation are slow movers of history, and new ones in the streets of Tokyo.

There is no question that most Japanese seek a new society with a new moral basis. The cynical, the intemperate, and the short-sighted would seize upon a solution that appears quick and effortless. But there is no such solution if a society wants everyone to be of value. On the issue of direct action, as the *Yomiuri* said the day after a student was killed in a Diet riot—a week and a half after the three papers had condoned the direct action of the illegal June 4 strike: "a country governed by law cannot allow a 'however'."

The three national papers, serving neither the Government nor the Opposition, should have recognized the dangers of "however" weeks before. A free press, one hopes, would be among the first to attack the narrow expediencies of two pitted factions. As all the papers pointed out, the primary issue of the Treaty struggle was not the Treaty or even the Kishi Government; it was parliamentarianism and democracy in Japan.

But since democracy is not an end to be achieved, rather a means that is itself the actuality, working in its name alone is not enough. Too late it is realized, as the press realized after the June 15 riot, that in political action the means of the present and the object of the future are theoretical terms describing the same process.

APPENDIX

Page 1 general news stories on the passage of the Treaty through the Lower House, May 20 morning editions. All italics have been added by the author.

Asahi

"The Diet on the night of the 19th, in connection with the extension of the Diet session and passage of the new Security Treaty, *fell into the most evil of conditions.* In the end Speaker of the Lower House Kiyose called in 500 policemen to use force in clearing out obstructionist Socialist Diet members and at 11:50 forced the opening of a Lower House plenary session. The Liberal-Democratic Party, with the Socialist and the Democratic-Socialist Diet members absent, then passed by itself a 50-day Diet extension.

"Then after this, the Opposition and Miki-Matsumura faction and other anti-mainstream Liberal-Democrats being absent, the Security Treaty and related agreements were put before the House. *They were passed wholesale.*

"The same night the Socialist and Democratic-Socialist Parties strongly emphasized that the decisions of the Special Lower House Committee for the Security Treaty and the plenary session were null and void. They said it had become absolutely necessary

Mainichi

"The problematic question of a Diet extension was settled last night in the midst of great disorder when the Liberal-Democratic Party voted it at 11:48. Five hundred policemen were used to expel the Socialist Diet members who were using force to block the opening of the special session. In the same way the controversial Security Treaty was passed just after midnight, the Miki-Matsumura and Ishibashi factions as well as the Opposition Parties being absent.

"Thus the Treaty will be automatically approved on the day of Ike's arrival, June 19th. However, the Socialists and Democratic-Socialists have stiffened their attitudes and the anti-main stream factions of the Liberal-Democratic Party are severely criticizing the action. Because of this the political situation has become unusually tense . . ."

[The article then gives a complete synopsis of the events of the morning and afternoon. Following is the description of the events leading to the vote.]

"Later the Socialist Diet members

Yomiuri

"The Liberal-Democratic Party's plan from the morning of the 19th to force a vote on Diet extension and the Security Treaty stiffened throughout the day as the Socialists, raising obstructions to the plan, fiercely defended themselves and tried to fight back. But, in accordance with Liberal-Democratic plans, Speaker Kiyose brought in the police after 11:00 to try to clear away the Socialist Diet members and their secretaries who were sitting in the corridor in front of the Speaker's office. The result of the free-for-all was that the Socialists were cleared out and the session opened at 11:50. The Liberal-Democratic Party, acting unilaterally, then voted through a Diet extension, and at 12:06, the Security Treaty and its related agreements."

[A synopsis of the day follows, somewhat less complete than the *Mainichi*'s.]

to defy the Government Party. They said that the tense state of affairs between the Government and Opposition Parties would continue. It appears that all Diet matters will be suspended."

[The article then gives a partial synopsis of the day's events. Following is the description of the events leading to the vote.]

"The bell announcing the opening of the Lower House plenary session sounded just after 10:30, but only the Liberal-Democratic Diet members went into the chamber. At 11:50 Speaker Kiyose at last went in. He opened the session and immediately had the extension voted on."

[In a separate story on P. 1 a description of the intervention of the police is given.]

"Entering the Lower House chambers from the South Gate, police at 11:07 on the 19th began to use force to uproot and completely clear out the Socialists sitting in the passageway in front of the Speaker's office. However, the Socialist Diet members resisted fiercely and the area was thrown into confusion. The use of force continued for about 20 minutes, but the police were unable to carry out *the job entrusted to them.*

"Finally the Liberal-Democrats grew impatient, and, in order to remove the Socialists, Diet Steering

(Continued in 3rd column)

and their secretaries sat down in the corridor in front of the Speaker's office. When the Liberal-Democratic secretaries asked them to leave a scuffle developed. Because of this Speaker Kiyose decided to call in police if necessary and at 9:55 announced over the loudspeaker system: 'Since you are not upholding order within the Diet, police will be brought in in 15 minutes if the corridors are not cleared.' Then at 10:35 the bell was rung announcing the opening of the plenary session.

"Since the Socialists still did not move, Speaker Kiyose again at 10:48 warned over the loudspeaker that the police would be brought in in 20 minutes."

Committee head Arafune and others took charge. It was their idea to get the Speaker through a door in his office to the Secretary-General's room, and from there to his chair in the Diet chamber. However, some Socialists had taken up a stand in the Speaker's anteroom and blocked the door with a screen. More police were called and the screen . . . was eventually destroyed.

"The police had by now cleared away the Socialists from in front of the Speaker's office, and, although the Socialists had wedged the door tightly shut, the police were able to force their way in. . . .

"Finally by 11:50 the police and Diet guards had cleared out the last of the Socialists from the passageway in front of the Speaker's office. Protected by this crowd, Speaker Kiyose, amid jeers from the Socialists and handshakes from the Liberal-Democratic Secretariat, passed through to the chamber and took his chair.

"As a result of this melee, the Speaker's ante-room and the Secretary-General's room had been nearly destroyed; everything had been stepped on and treated violently. *The Diet showed for the first time what its wretched condition was going to be in the future.*"

Page 11 stories on the use of the police, May 20 morning editions.

Asahi

"Policemen dressed in gray uniforms silently climbed onto the red carpet of the Diet last night. For the first time since the Diet riots of 1954 and 1956 they have left *their disgusting stain* on the Diet. It was the end of the session on the Treaty; *the public's expectations were completely betrayed. 'Serious debate' proved to be a lie.*

"In order to force a Diet extension, the Liberal-Democrats *used the police as a tool* to oust Socialist Diet members who were holding a sit-down strike in front of the Speaker's office. *Spirited cries* of 'wassho, wassho' rose in the Diet against the police. Outside the windows the voices of demonstrators opposing the Treaty echoed under the dark sky . . .

"They pulled away the Socialist Diet members with exactly the same methods they would have used with Zengakuren demonstrators. *The terrible police* trampled on the red rug and attacked. With a roar the corridor was cleared. The Socialists were dragged out with their arms pinned to their sides, their shirts torn, their neckties off, their hair flying. Four had to be carried out bodily by the police.

"As they were dragged off one by

Mainichi

"Both inside and outside the Diet building the drama of the 'Security Treaty session' reached its climax on the night of the 19th. The last act saw the police used and the Diet shaken with violent political storms.

"Inside the Diet, while the Government and Opposition Parties were shouting with anger at each other, police uprooted the 'picketing' Socialists. The Liberal-Democratic Party by itself then forced a plenary session. Outside the Diet in the rain about 25,000 labor unionists and students demonstrated against the Treaty.

"With attitudes both inside and outside of the Diet too violent to allow compromises, the Liberal-Democrats cut off discussion on the new Treaty. Six Socialist Diet members and 45 policemen were injured.

"Three lines of policemen at 11:05 passed through the gate to the Lower House. Then the police entered—The mass of gray uniforms and hats silently climbed the stairs and went to the Speaker's office. In the third stain on the Diet since the war, the Liberal-Democrats welcomed them as they passed, shaking hands and telling them to 'take courage!'

"The Socialist Diet members who were trying to block a plenary session

Yomiuri

"Even blue-uniformed police were called into the chalk-walled 'midnight Diet' on the 19th where the new Treaty was being considered. A violent political storm shook the Diet. Stepping onto the red rug, policemen pulled out one by one the Socialist Diet members and their secretaries who were sitting in front of the Speaker's office. There was a swirl of angry, rejecting shouts. It was the kind of amazing confusion that makes one ask, 'Is this a Diet of good sense?'

"Outside 30,000 demonstrators seemed about to force their way into the Diet at any time . . .

"The road to the new Security Treaty was opened when the four-meter distance separating the Speaker's ante-room from the plenary chamber was opened. At about 10:00 some 300 Socialist Diet members and secretaries had sat down across the 'road' and filled the corridor. At 10:50 Speaker Kiyose announced over the loudspeaker, 'Please clear the way; if you do not do so in five minutes I will use police.' But the Socialist Diet members, 'expanding their bodies,' did not move one step. Then at about 11:03, some 500 policemen began to come in from downstairs."

one *they were heckled in a despicable way* by those in the 'spectator seats' on the stairways. 'Why don't they put them in handcuffs?' and other things were yelled at their backs. 'What kind of behavior is this?' one would ask. And in fact most of the hecklers wore badges saying they were secretaries to Liberal-Democrats.

"The Socialist Diet members had pinned white roses to their chests as symbols of peace, but these white roses were trampled into the red carpet, *symbolized the way the authority of the Diet had been smeared with mud.* Were the white gloves the police wore when they attacked supposed to absolve them from this?"

by barricading the Speaker's office were ousted to the last man by *the crushing strength of the police. The* cries of 'down with the Treaty' from the demonstrators surrounding the Diet building bounced off the chalk building. The police, their night sticks and pistols unfastened, put their white gloves on their waists and lined up in front of the Speaker's office.

"'Return to your barracks!' 'Is this Rhee's parliament?' the Socialists yelled, and at once the ousting began."